Congressional
Pay and Perquisites

Date Due

Congressional Pay and Perquisites

History, Facts, and Controversy

CONGRESSIONAL QUARTERLY, INC.
WASHINGTON, D.C.

Photos: 2, 20, 49, 76—R. Michael Jenkins; 9—Paul Conklin; 12—Karen Ruckman; 22, 83—Teresa Zabala; 38—Marty La Vor; 61, 66, 71—Library of Congress; 79—Ken Heinen

Printed in the United States of America

Library of Congress Cataloging-in-Publication Data

Congressional pay and perquisites : history, facts, and controversy.

     p. cm.
    Includes bibliographical references and index.
    ISBN 0-87187-627-2
    1. United States. Congress--Salaries,
    etc. 2. United States.
Congress--Salaries, etc.--History. I. Congressional Quarterly Inc.
JK781.C66 1992
328.73'0068'3--dc20
                         92-4087
                           CIP

Editor: Mary W. Cohn
Contributors: Marty Gottron, Kerry Kern, Nancy Kervin, Jenny K. Philipson, Amy Stern
Book Design: Kaelin Chappell

CONTENTS

Preface

In 1789 members of Congress were paid a flat rate of $6 per working day, from which they had to pay their living expenses, incidental expenses related to their congressional work, and out-of-town living costs. Congressional salaries rose very gradually throughout the 19th century and were only as high as $10,000 a year by 1946. Since then, salaries have increased more than twelvefold, to $125,100 a year in 1991.

In the early years of Congress senators and representatives had no staff and no expense accounts. Now there are nearly twenty thousand aides who work directly for Congress. And, according to one study, in 1991 each senator cost the taxpayer $4.6 million annually and each representative cost $1.6 million.

Congress clearly needs a skilled staff, facilities, and information systems to assist members in dealing with the mounting volume of legislation and constituent demands. But congressional pay and perks have recently come under scrutiny as never before, and members are battling to protect their image—and their political lives. Voters are furious with what they perceive as large congressional pay raises, with scandals involving members' check kiting and unpaid restaurant tabs, with foreign junkets taken at taxpayer expense, and with the influence they believe congressional staff wield. The media are publicizing the fringe benefits lawmakers enjoy, from discounted barber shops and beauty parlors to travel expense accounts to the use of radio and television recording studios at less than commercial rates.

Now members fear that the electorate's simmering resentment against incumbents may boil over, burn them individually, and damage Congress's already battered image. In a sense, members of Congress are paying a price for their pay and perks.

How This Book Is Organized

Congressional Pay and Perquisites provides a chronological account of the pay and honoraria system and describes the various perks provided to members.

Chapter 1 covers pay levels for members of Congress since 1789, including the battles over raises that have been fought over the years.

The honoraria system is discussed in Chapter 2. Congress's gradual abolishment of honoraria payments is traced.

One of the most controversial perks for incumbents—the franking privilege—is explored in Chapter 3. Included is information on what types of materials may be franked as well as recent changes made to the franking system to make individual members more accountable for mailing costs.

Chapter 4 focuses on foreign travel. To the member who travels, the trip is a fact-finding mission; to critics, these trips are junkets at the taxpayers' expense.

Office allowances—money used to set up a congressional office, pay phone and domestic travel bills, buy stationery, print and mail newsletters, and hire staff—are described in Chapter 5.

Additional benefits members enjoy, such as life and health insurance, swimming pools and gyms, recording studios, and Capitol Hill restaurants, are spelled out in Chapter 6.

Chapter 7 covers political patronage. This perk is no longer considered as important as it once was.

Congressional staff have often been called the unelected representatives of Congress. The growth, makeup, and power of staff are discussed in Chapter 8.

The information in this volume first appeared in *Guide to Congress,* 4th ed.

CHAPTER 1

Congressional Pay:
Perennial Political Issue

Disputes over pay and benefits have been a constant feature of congressional politics throughout the nation's history. The American public is perennially unconvinced that senators and representatives are underpaid, and fights over pay increases inevitably provoke blunt displays of public scorn. Congress's first pay raise, in 1816, had to be repealed after many members were driven from office by public outcry.

Fear of criticism from the voters made members of Congress skittish about voting to increase their own pay, even when their salaries failed to keep up with inflation. Over the years they found ingenious ways to increase their income without having to cast a direct vote on a pay raise. These steps included using independent commissions to set pay levels, providing tax deductions for members' Washington living expenses, and participating in automatic salary increases established for federal workers.

Until the practice was banned in 1991, many lawmakers augmented their government salaries with honoraria—speaking fees and other payments from private interests. Members of Congress collected more than $9 million in honoraria in 1989.

The widespread practice of making speeches for honoraria was assailed as, at best, a source of distraction from the business of government and, at worst, a form of legalized bribery. Criticism of honoraria mounted through the 1980s, as outside interests became more and more brazen about using the payments to gain access to members of Congress. Stories of politicians picking up a $2,000 check for dropping by at a breakfast increasingly tainted the whole system.

A spate of congressional scandals in the late 1980s gave new impetus to proposals to curb outside income. In 1989 the House voted to ban honoraria as of 1991 and hiked representatives' pay to $125,100 to make up for the financial loss. The Senate refused to go along immediately, but in 1991 it also adopted the ban on honoraria and boosted its pay to the $125,100 House level.

SETTING CONGRESSIONAL SALARIES

Article I, Section 6 of the Constitution provides that "Senators and Representatives shall receive a Compensation for their Services, to be ascertained by Law, and paid out of the Treasury of the United States."

R. Michael Jenkins

Members of Congress have always been skittish about raising their own pay because constituents inevitably complain. In 1989 Rep. Dan Rostenkowski offered an emotional defense of a House pay raise proposal: "I am proud of what I do and you, my colleagues, should feel the same way," he said.

The constitutional language settled one sensitive contemporary issue—whether a member's salary should be drawn from state or national funds—but it left the resolution of a far more delicate question up to Congress itself—deciding what that salary should be. The inevitable result was to make congressional salaries a political issue that has plagued Congress throughout its history.

In trying to minimize the adverse political fallout from periodically raising its own salary, Congress fell into the practice of incorporating such pay increases in general pay legislation granting raises for most government workers, including at times the judiciary and the president. But even that tactic often failed to blunt critical reaction.

Public opposition to congressional pay increases has been particularly strong at various times in the nation's history, leading to wholesale election defeats of members who voted for increases their constituents considered unwarranted. On two occasions controversial salary increases were repealed by succeeding Congresses. Frequently, a few members refuse their pay raises, returning the increase to the Treasury or donating it to a public charity. Technically, all members must accept full pay. After receiving their salary, however, they may return any portion to the Treasury.

Despite the resistance both within and outside Congress, congressional pay has risen steadily, particularly in recent years. A member's pay in 1789 was $6 a day; by 1991 it had risen to $125,100 a year. Although the salary of members remained unchanged for long periods, only rarely was it reduced. The last salary cut was during the Depression years of 1933-35.

EARLY PAY LEGISLATION

During the Constitutional Convention of 1787 a principal question surrounding compensation of members was the source of the funds. Members of Congress under the Articles of Confederation had been paid by the states (members of the British Parliament at that time were not compensated). It was felt, however, that members of Congress under the Constitution should be paid, and paid by the national government.

Another question raised at the convention was whether senators and representatives should receive equal pay. Charles Pinckney of South Carolina twice moved "that no salary should be allowed" members of the Senate. "As this branch was meant to represent the wealth of the country," Pinckney asserted, "it ought to be composed of persons of wealth; and if no allowance was to be made, the wealthy alone would undertake the service." Pinckney's motion was seconded by

Benjamin Franklin but twice was rejected, by votes of six states to five.[1]

Per Diem Compensation

One of the first, and most controversial, measures enacted by the new Congress in 1789 was a bill fixing the compensation of members. As originally approved by the House, representatives and senators alike were to be paid $6 a day. The proposal for equal pay developed into a dispute over whether senators, by reason of greater responsibilities and presumably higher qualifications, should receive a pay differential.

At the heart of the debate was an amendment by Rep. Theodore Sedgwick, a Massachusetts Federalist, to lower House pay to $5 a day, thus creating a $1-a-day differential in favor of senators. But the amendment was defeated by voice vote. On August 10, 1789, the House by a 30-16 roll call passed a bill providing for payment of $6 a day to members of both chambers.

In the Senate the bill was amended to provide that senators be paid at the $6 rate until March 4, 1795, when their pay would be increased to $8 a day; the pay of representatives would remain at $6. The amended bill passed the Senate on August 28, 1789.

After a House-Senate conference on the issue, the House on September 11 by a 29-25 vote agreed to fix the pay of senators at $7 a day after March 4, 1795, and by a 28-26 vote set March 4, 1796, as the expiration date of the legislation. The Senate agreed to the House amendments on September 12, and the bill was signed into law on September 22, 1789, seven days before the end of the first session of Congress.

As enacted, the measure provided the first congressional perquisite: a travel allowance for senators and representatives of $6 for each twenty miles. It also provided a $6-a-day differential for the House Speaker (making his pay $12 a day) and compensation for a number of lesser House and Senate officials.

When a new pay law was enacted in 1796, only a glancing reference was made to continuing the differential for the Senate. Both the House and the Senate passed a bill equalizing the pay at $6 a day.

Short-Lived Salary Law

In 1816 Congress voted itself a pay increase and a shift from per diem compensation to an annual salary. An act of March 19, 1816, raised congressional pay to $1,500 a year and made the raise retroactive to December 4, 1815, when the first session of the 14th Congress convened. The pay raise had been passed easily by both houses, but it was roundly condemned by the population at large. A number of members who had voted for the bill were defeated in the 1816 general election, and nine members resigned over the issue. One of the election victims was Rep. Daniel Webster, a New Hampshire Federalist. He was not elected to Congress again until 1822.

The short session of the 14th Congress in 1817 repealed the $1,500 salary act, effective at the end of that Congress March 3, 1817. An act of January 22, 1818, restored per diem compensation and set the rate at $8, retroactive to March 3, 1817.

1850s-1930s

Almost four decades after Congress had returned to per diem compensation, a successful conversion to annual congressional salaries finally was achieved. An act of August 16, 1856, replaced the $8-a-day rate with a $3,000 annual salary, retroactive to the start of the 34th Congress December 3, 1855. Another retroactive pay increase—to $5,000—was approved July 28, 1866, and made effective as of December 4, 1865, when the 39th Congress convened for its first session.

In the closing days of the 42nd Congress in 1873, still another retroactive pay raise was enacted, increasing salaries to $7,500. The higher salary was made retroactive to the beginning of the 42nd Congress, in effect providing members with a $5,000 windfall ($2,500 per year for the two preceding years). Despite precedents for making the increase retroactive, the size of the increase and the windfall effect boomeranged. Criticism of Congress already was at a high level because of the Crédit Mobilier scandal, and the pay increase was immediately condemned as a "salary grab" and a "back-pay steal." Some members returned their pay to the Treasury; others donated it to colleges or charities.

When the 43rd Congress opened in December 1873, scores of bills were introduced to repeal the increase. By an act of January 20, 1874, congressional pay reverted to the previous $5,000 annual rate, where it stayed until a $7,500 salary was sanctioned in February 1907. A raise to $10,000 was approved in March 1925.

Government austerity was the byword as the Great Depression of the 1930s deepened. Salaries of federal employees were reduced, and members of Congress likewise had to take a pay cut. The Economy Act of June 30, 1932, provided for a 10 percent cutback in members' salaries, dropping them from $10,000 to $9,000. The cutback was increased another 5 percent, meaning a further drop to $8,500, by the Economy Act of March 20, 1933. Gradually the cutbacks were rescinded, and by the end of 1935 congressional salaries had been restored to the $10,000 level.

1940s-1960s

No further salary changes occurred until passage of the Legislative Reorganization Act of 1946, which increased congressional salaries from $10,000 to $12,500 and retained an existing $2,500 nontaxable expense allowance for all members. The increase took effect at the beginning of the 80th Congress in 1947. A $15,000 annual salary and elimination of the expense allowance had been recommended in committee, but the legislation was amended in the House, and the House provision was retained in the final version of the act. The measure provided $20,000 salaries for the vice president and Speaker of the House.[2]

Expense Allowance Controversy

Provision for the $2,500 expense allowance for representatives had been made in 1945 when the House Appropriations Committee included funding for it in a legislative branch appropriations bill. Although the bill did not so stipulate, the committee said the allowance probably would be tax-exempt. When the measure reached the House floor, opponents called the allowance an opening wedge for inflation and a pay increase by subterfuge. But a special rule drafted by the Rules Committee waived all points of order against the bill, thus thwarting efforts to eliminate the allowance on the floor. The legislation subsequently was adopted, 229-124. Other attempts to eliminate or change the proposal also failed, and the House approved the bill.

The Senate Appropriations Committee reported the bill after adding a $2,500 expense allowance for senators. But the committee amendment was defeated by the Senate, 9-43, and two compromise amendments also failed. An amendment to delete the House expense allowance was narrowly defeated, 22-28. The Senate thus passed the bill, which later was enacted, with the allowance for representatives but not for senators.

The question came up again during Senate action on a fiscal 1946 supplemental appropriations bill. The Senate committee offered an amendment to extend the expense allowance to senators, but the Senate again rejected the plan, 24-47.

Senators ultimately received the $2,500 expense allowance in 1946 through the fiscal 1947 legislative branch appropriations bill.

In the Revenue Act of 1951 Congress eliminated the tax-free expense allowances, effective January 3, 1952. Also made subject to taxation were the expense allowances of the president, vice president, and Speaker of the House.

Congress in 1953 created a Commission on Judicial and Congressional Salaries to study the salary question and make recommendations to Congress. As approved by the Senate, the commission would have been empowered to raise salaries, but the House amended the measure to require congressional approval for any pay increase. The commission's report recommended a $10,000 salary boost, but Congress took no action.

In 1955, however, Congress enacted legislation raising both congressional and judicial salaries. The bill increased members' salaries to $22,500 (from $12,500 plus the $2,500 expense allowance). It also provided $35,000 for the Speaker and the vice president (up from $30,000) and retained the existing $10,000 taxable expense allowance for both positions. The increases became effective March 1, 1955.

The chief difference between the House and Senate bills was over the $2,500 expense allowance, which the House wanted to retain. But the Senate deleted it. Then the Senate rejected the final conference version because it retained an expense allowance provision. After that provision had been deleted, a second conference bill without the allowance was approved by Congress.

In 1964 Congress again approved raises in its own salaries, and those of other federal government employees. Members' salaries were raised by $7,500, to $30,000, effective in 1965. Salaries of the Speaker and the vice president were raised to $43,000. The bill was enacted after the House first killed a version of the bill raising congressional salaries by $10,000. The second measure was strongly backed by President Lyndon B. Johnson. Congress acted on the bill after most of the 1964 congressional primary elections had been held. It was passed in the House by a vote of 243-157 and in the Senate by 58-21.

Automatic Salary Increases

In 1967 Congress established a nine-member Commission on Executive, Legislative, and Judicial Salaries to review the salaries of members of Congress, federal judges, and top officers of the executive branch every four years and to recommend changes.

Creation of the commission plan was designed to relieve members of Congress of the politically risky task of periodically having to raise their own salaries. And it was hoped that the commission would set the salaries of top officials high enough to attract and keep the best qualified persons.

Three members of the commission were to be appointed by the president, two by the president of the Senate, two by the Speaker of the House, and two by the chief justice. Beginning in fiscal 1969, the commission was to submit its recommendations to the president, who was to propose in his annual budget message the exact rates of pay "he deems advisable" for federal executives, judges, and members of Congress. His recommendations could be either higher or lower than those of the commission, or he could propose that salaries not be altered. The recommendations were to take effect within thirty days unless Congress either disapproved all or part of the recommendations or enacted a separate pay measure.

The law did not work as well as its sponsors had hoped, although in its first test, in 1969, it worked as planned. Congressional salaries were increased from $30,000 to $42,500. But in 1973 President Richard Nixon delayed naming a pay commission, and pay proposals were not sent to Congress until 1974, an election year. The Senate,

Remedy for Absenteeism: Docking Members' Pay

One suggestion as a way to curb absenteeism in Congress is to dock a member's pay for each day he fails to appear on the floor of the House or Senate. The Constitution makes no provision for this, saying only that "each House shall be the Judge of the Elections, Returns and Qualifications of its own Members, and a Majority of each shall constitute a Quorum to do Business; but a smaller Number may adjourn from day to day, and may be authorized to compel the Attendance of absent Members, in such Manner, and under such Penalties as each House may provide." (Article 1, Section 5)

Nevertheless, the first session of the First Congress in 1789 provided for an automatic docking of pay. Salaries were $6 a day for each day of attendance.

A law enacted in 1856 provided that "the Secretary of the Senate and the Sergeant at Arms of the House, respectively, shall deduct from the monthly payments of each member or delegate the amount of his salary for each day that he has been absent from the Senate or House, ... unless such member or delegate assigns as the reason for such absence the sickness of himself or of some member of his family."

Since then a few isolated attempts to compel attendance have cited this law. During the 53rd Congress in 1894, after a ruling of the chair that the 1856 law was still in force, portions of some House members' salaries were withheld.

The 1894 incident was recalled in 1914 when the House adopted a resolution revoking all leaves of absence granted to members and directing the sergeant at arms to reduce members' pay for each day they were absent. The 1914 resolution was enforced stringently for a brief time.

But soon the practice of docking a member's pay for absenteeism was abandoned. The House parliamentarian's office argued there was no way of knowing when a member was away from his official duties.

In 1975 the Senate inserted a provision repealing the 1856 law in the fiscal 1976 legislative branch appropriations bill, but it was dropped from the final version of that bill.

In 1981 a U.S. district court judge rejected a California taxpayer's complaint that federal lawmakers should not be paid for days when they are absent from Congress without an excuse. In a brief opinion, Judge Spencer Williams of the Northern District of California dismissed the suit, ruling that merely being a taxpayer did not give the Californian sufficient standing to file the suit. Williams added that it would be "inappropriate for the courts to inquire into or supervise the attendance of members of a coordinate branch of government."

In a similar 1972 suit, a federal judge had dismissed a suit seeking to recover salaries and allowances paid several members of Congress who were away from Washington campaigning for the presidency.

---

uneasy about a pay raise at that time, killed the proposed increases.

1975-1991

Congressional salaries were not increased again for almost seven years, during which period the cost of living had risen 47.5 percent. But in 1975, Congress, with sleight of hand, approved a pay raise for itself and other top officials of the government. Congress opted to make itself and other top officials eligible for the annual governmentwide pay increase, which was designed to maintain pay comparability between government workers and those in the private sector. The increase would be received automatically unless members of the House or Senate decided not to take it.

The plan was worked out secretly over several months by congressional leaders in consultation with the Ford administration. It was cleared by Congress only five days after most members had first heard of it. One representative called the debate "vicious, one of the ugliest, most disgusting things I've ever seen. . . . Members who rarely say a thing during floor debate were shouting and screaming at each other, saying, 'Don't be a hero, you want this raise as much as we do.' It was ugly."

The result was a 5 percent pay increase for members, bringing congressional salaries to $44,600 annually. The raise was much criticized by the voters, and in 1976 Congress decided it was prudent to pass up the automatic increase for that year. A provision denying the comparability pay raise to members of Congress was added to the fiscal 1977 legislative branch appropriations bill.

1977 Pay Raise

Congress in 1977 made up for lost time by giving itself and other top government officials of the executive, legislative, and judicial branches a $12,900 pay raise, increasing lawmakers' salaries to $57,500 annually. This amounted to a pay hike of about 29 percent. It was the first increase in basic pay since 1969.

The raise had been recommended by the third quadrennial Commission on Executive, Legislative, and Judicial Salaries, chaired by businessman Peter G. Peterson. It conditioned its proposals for a salary increase upon adoption of a strong ethics code governing congressional conduct. And the panel called for public disclosure of members' financial worth, rigorous restrictions on outside earned income and on potential conflicts of interest, fully accountable expense allowances, and publicly reported auditing of the ethics codes' provisions.

Repeal of Automatic Procedure. Senators and representatives paid a price when they raised their salaries that year. Congress repealed the procedure that had allowed raises to take effect without a congressional vote. And the new ethics codes adopted by both chambers as part of the 1977 pay increase negotiations included a ban on so-called slush funds—unofficial office accounts maintained with cash gifts from members' friends and supporters—and tight limits on outside income. (In 1979, however, the Senate suspended those outside income limits for four years.)

Congress also denied itself the scheduled 1977 comparability increase. Even so, criticism of the earlier raise that year was widespread.

In 1978 Congress also voted to forgo that year's comparability increase. Also affected were the top congressional aides, judges, and all other federal officials at or over the $47,500 pay level. Some sixteen thousand persons were affected. Other federal workers got the raise, which was 5.5 percent.

1977 Tax Break. Congress cleared legislation in July 1977 exempting members of Congress from paying income taxes in those jurisdictions where they lived while attending sessions of Congress. A similar bill was passed by Congress in 1976 but was vetoed by President Gerald R. Ford on grounds that it unfairly created a special class of citizens with special privileges.

The 1977 tax exemption was challenged in the courts, but it was upheld by the Supreme Court in 1981.

As a practical matter, Maryland was the only state affected by the law because Virginia and the District of Columbia already had exempted members of Congress from their income tax laws. In 1977 there were about 125 members living in Maryland, and that number of members was estimated to be living there when the Supreme Court upheld the law in 1981.

1979 Senate-House Feud

The political sensitivity of congressional pay was apparent once again in 1979 when the issue set off a Senate-House feud. That dispute forced the government to begin fiscal 1980 without spending authority for many federal agencies.

As 1979 began, members were earning $57,500 a year. Moreover, they were due for a 7 percent pay hike that October under the comparability pay procedures then in effect. Under the 1975 salary law Congress was automatically entitled to the annual raise granted federal employees, unless it voted to block the increase.

Besides the proposed 7 percent increase, members hoped to recoup the 5.5 percent comparability adjustment from 1978 that Congress had voted not to take in that election year. The 1978 hike had not been repealed; it had just been suspended for a year. Thus if Congress took no action on it, members would receive both pay hikes, plus interest on the 5.5 percent raise, for a total increase of 12.9 percent, or more than $7,400.

With another election just a year away, however, a move was launched to limit or deny the congressional pay hikes altogether. Also caught up in the politics of the pay issue were federal judges and top-level executive branch bureaucrats making at least $47,500; past pay freezes had covered them as well.

The House Appropriations Committee recommended that the raise be limited to 7 percent, but in June the House knocked that limit down to 5.5 percent and then rejected the appropriations bill because it thought that increase too high.

Then, in late September, Congress became bogged down over an emergency stopgap funding bill that was being used as the vehicle for the pay hike. That measure was needed to fund agencies whose regular appropriations bills had not yet been approved. The House, in a nonrecorded vote, accepted a compromise 5.5 percent hike. The

Senate knocked that out and said "no raise."

But just two days before the new fiscal year was to begin, the House insisted on the raise and adjourned for a week's recess, leaving the Senate with an unenviable choice: It could either approve the emergency funding resolution, thus keeping the government in business but also accepting the 5.5 percent pay increase, or kill the funding resolution, thus permitting the automatic 12.9 percent increase to go into effect but depriving most of the government of authority to spend money as of October 1. An angry Senate voted to kill the resolution.

Finally, on October 12, almost two weeks after the new fiscal year had begun and just before thousands of federal workers were about to be denied a paycheck, Congress approved an emergency funding measure that rolled back the 12.9 percent increase to 5.5 percent. The new raise brought congressional salaries up to $60,663 beginning in 1980.

While the increases for members of Congress and top executive branch officials were rolled back, federal judges were able to retain the entire 12.9 percent pay hike because under the Constitution Congress is prohibited from reducing the compensation of judges during their term of office.

1980-1981 Pay Controversies

In 1980 Congress denied itself a 9.11 percent comparability increase that President Jimmy Carter had recommended for federal workers. The following year lawmakers included a provision prohibiting the pay adjustment in a fiscal 1981 continuing appropriations bill. The prohibition was extended through the end of fiscal 1981 in two subsequent laws.[3]

In 1981, citing the need to cut federal spending, Congress rejected another large pay raise—amounting to 16.8 percent—for lawmakers and high-level government employees. (President Carter in 1980 had recommended a pay raise to

$70,853 based on the recommendation of the Commission on Executive, Legislative, and Judicial Salaries. President Ronald Reagan, who originally supported the increase, changed his mind, citing budgetary considerations.)

The proposed 1981 pay raise was debated amid disagreement between House and Senate members over the proper procedure for acting on proposed congressional salary hikes. The House and Senate each followed a different path in rejecting the pay raise. The Senate took a recorded vote on four separate resolutions of disapproval; the House merely took a voice vote on a resolution affirming "the sense of the House."

In 1977 Congress had amended the 1969 pay law by requiring each house to approve a presidential pay recommendation within sixty days in order for the proposed increase to take effect. The amendment stated that each chamber must take recorded votes on raising the pay of each branch of government. The approval of both chambers was required to raise the pay of employees in any of the three branches of government.

Paul Conklin

Sen. Ted Stevens, R-Alaska, is a longtime champion of increased congressional salaries and benefits. Most members scurry for cover when the subject of pay raises comes up.

1982: Future Automatic Raises

Congress had hoped to avoid controversy by voting in 1975 to make itself eligible for the automatic annual comparability pay raise granted federal employees. But because Congress had to appropriate the funds each year for its raise, the issue came up annually. In an effort to further depoliticize congressional pay, lawmakers voted to fund congressional salaries through a permanent appropriation, effective October 1982. The new pay procedure was approved in October 1981 as a rider attached to an emergency funding bill. The move eliminated one avenue for rejecting the annual raise, but members opposed to congressional pay hikes continued to find ways to bring up the pay raise issue.

The final version of that legislation did not contain a 4.8 percent congressional pay raise for 1981 sought by House members.

1981: Tax Deductions

In the same 1981 emergency appropriations bill containing the comparability adjustment procedure, Congress approved a change in congressional tax laws that enabled senators and representatives to deduct from their income taxes the expenses they incurred while residing in Washington. Under a 1952 law members had been allowed a maximum deduction of $3,000.

The Joint Taxation Committee estimated in 1981 that the change would cost the Treasury $3 million a year and provide a typical member in the 45 percent tax bracket with the equivalent of a $10,500 pay raise.

Though a similar proposal was pushed earlier in 1981 by House Appropriations Committee Chairman Jamie L. Whitten, D-Miss., it never came to a vote in the House. But Sen. Ted Stevens, R-Alaska, won approval of the plan in the Senate. Besides the tax deduction change, Stevens had shepherded through to enactment measures increasing legislators' official perquisites, loosening restrictions on outside earnings by lawmakers, and modifying provisions of the Senate's ethics code that placed strict limits on senators' honoraria.

Resolving Conflicting Statutes. After the tax change had been enacted, it was discovered that the new deductions conflicted with a provision of a 1976 statute limiting the amount of deductions a person living alone could take on second homes used in connection with a trade or business.

Under the combined effect of the 1976 and 1981 laws, a member of Congress who lived alone while working in Washington could, in the same tax year, depreciate the cost of a second home in the capital area as well as deduct from his taxes his Washington housing expenses. But a member whose family resided with him in Washington for more than fourteen days a year was not eligible for both tax breaks.

To remedy the situation Congress in December 1981 tacked a nongermane tax provision onto an unrelated bill and passed that measure without a roll-call vote. The bill enabled members living with their families in Washington to claim the same tax benefits as members living alone. Congress also instructed the Treasury secretary to prescribe the "appropriate" business deduction a member could take for each day Congress was in session without actually having to substantiate his business expenses.

Treasury Ruling for 1981. Under regulations approved by the Treasury in January 1982, the 1981 deduction would result in a saving of at least $19,200 for senators and $19,650 for House members. Since previous law allowed members a maximum deduction of $3,000 a year for their Washington expenses, the new legislation provided an additional deduction of at least $16,200 for senators and $16,650 for House members for that year. (The deduction would vary from year to year, depending on how many days each house was in session.)

A married member with two children and typical deductions who lived on his congressional salary alone during 1981 was able to keep about $7,000 that otherwise would have been paid in taxes, according to Congressional Quarterly calculations based on figures supplied by the Internal Revenue Service. Members with high Washington living expenses or with outside incomes in addition to their salaries could qualify for even bigger tax breaks.

1982: Tax Deduction Repeal

The tax breaks provoked a public outcry. Taxpayers flooded Capitol Hill and the Internal Revenue Service with angry letters and phone calls protesting the new deductions. Common Cause, the citizens' lobby group, criticized the tax deductions as unjustified and inequitable and launched a nationwide "Give Taxpayers A Break" campaign to repeal the 1981 tax deduction. It pledged to get all representatives and senators to publicly disclose the amount of the deductions for Washington living expenses they took in 1981. According to Common Cause President Fred Wertheimer, "Congress's failure to provide regular cost-of-living adjustments for itself cannot justify enacting extravagant and unjustified tax breaks that turn members of Congress into a privileged class of taxpayers. This is bound to undermine public confidence in the fairness of our tax system."

In response to the pressure, Congress in 1982 approved legislation repealing the 1981 deductions. The measure was enacted into law July 18, but was made retroactive to January 1. It nevertheless allowed members to keep the lucrative deductions they took on their 1981 tax returns. The repeal restored the $3,000 annual limit on a member's deductions for Washington expenses—the limit that had been in force before 1981. The repeal, initiated by Sen. William Proxmire, D-Wis., was tacked onto a fiscal 1982 supplemental appropriations bill for federal agencies.

Earlier that year, the House threatened not to approve the repeal unless senators agreed to limit their outside earned income to the maximum allowed representatives. That dispute stalled final action on the spending bill/tax deduction repeal and exacerbated a bitter struggle between the House and Senate over the twin issues of members' tax breaks and honoraria. But the House backed down when it looked as if the honoraria provision might tie up the funding bill indefinitely.

1982: Pay Differential

Breaking nearly two hundred years of tradition, Congress ended its 97th term with House members earning higher salaries than senators. But at the same time the Senate repealed a rule that would have limited outside earnings, thus allowing senators to earn as much as they wanted from business income, legal fees, and honoraria for appearances and speeches.

The changes in pay and honoraria were enacted in 1982 during a lame duck session, after members initially shunned a preelection salary increase. With help from members who did not have to worry about reelection, the House in December approved a 15 percent pay raise, increasing representatives' pay to $69,800 as of December 18.

The Senate rejected the pay raise but voted to kill a cap on outside earnings, passed in 1977 and scheduled to take effect January 1, 1983. Outside earnings for House members remained limited to

30 percent of a representative's salary—$20,940.

In 1981 some senators had earned as much as $48,000 in honoraria, leading some House members to remark that the Senate actually got a better arrangement.

Preelection Jitters. Before the November election the House turned back initial attempts by the Senate to raise congressional salaries. On August 17, House members rejected, 266-145, a conference report on a budget reconciliation bill because it contained a provision that would have required the Commission on Executive, Legislative, and Judicial Salaries to convene a special session and recommend a congressional pay increase by November 15. Congress would then have had thirty days to reject the raise or it would have taken effect.

The Senate went along with the House, and the offending provision was removed before the reconciliation bill was enacted.

On August 18 the House also killed, by voice vote, an identical provision that had been inserted in a fiscal 1982 supplemental appropriations bill.

The upcoming elections had members particularly gun-shy. Said Rep. Vic Fazio, D-Calif., "Obviously, we are in an election period, and it is not a good time to talk about these things."

But Rep. Ken Holland, D-S.C., who was leaving Congress because of the pay, said, "Somebody like me with four children, the first beginning college next week, just cannot remain in Washington under the pay that is provided."

As the elections drew closer, members also voted to forgo a 4 percent increase recommended by President Reagan for federal workers. Under a 1975 law, members of Congress were slated to get the same comparability raise as federal employees. But in September Congress included a provision in a stopgap budget measure that barred lawmakers and senior bureaucrats from getting the increase, which took effect October 1.

Rep. Ken Holland, D-S.C., left Congress after four terms because "somebody like me with four children . . . just cannot remain in Washington under the pay that is provided."

Final Action. Both the House pay increase and the Senate change in honoraria were included in the final fiscal 1983 continuing appropriations measure, cleared by Congress December 20. The legislation made the $9,138 House raise effective December 18. The House voted 303-109 for the increase, but the key vote came when members rejected an amendment to keep pay at the existing level. The amendment failed 208-208, with outgoing Rep. Robert K. Dornan, R-Calif., casting the tying no vote and seventy other lame ducks also voting no.

The House also added a section limiting all members of Congress to outside earnings of 30 percent. The Senate deleted the pay raise and the outside earnings cap. The compromise resulted in a salary increase for House members and no limit on outside earnings for senators.

1983: Pay-Honoraria Dispute

In 1983, six months after the House had voted itself a 15 percent pay raise, senators followed suit, accepting a $9,138 increase effective July 1. That brought both House and Senate salaries to $69,800 a year.

Senators also agreed to limit their honoraria earnings to 30 percent of their salaries, the same amount House members could earn in total outside income. The limit on honoraria would take effect January 1, 1984. The change in Senate pay and honoraria was included in a fiscal 1983 supplemental appropriations bill that cleared Congress July 29.

The pay raise arose out of an attempt by House members to limit senators' honoraria earnings. When 1982 figures revealed that more than half of the Senate took in honoraria totaling more than 30 percent of their salaries and that some senators' honoraria earnings exceeded their salaries, outraged House members slapped a 30 percent limit on the amount senators could earn in speaking and writing fees. *(Honoraria, p. 21)*

The amendment, added during the House Appropriations Committee's markup of the fiscal 1983 supplemental bill, was not contested during House floor debate.

The issue, however, impeded Senate action on the bill until Senate leaders worked out an agreement. During the pay raise debate, senators were forced to vote on a variety of options and at one point agreed 51-41 to cap honoraria without raising annual salaries. One week later senators approved, 49-47, an amendment limiting honoraria to 30 percent of their salaries and increasing Senate pay to $69,800.

1984: "Backdoor" Increase

In 1984 congressional salaries rose from $69,800 to $72,600, despite an overwhelming Senate vote to

Congressional Pay

Year	Salary	Year	Salary
1789-1795	$6 per diem	December 1982-1983	$69,800 per year (House)
1795-1796	$6 per diem (House)	July 1983	$69,800 per year (Senate)
	$7 per diem (Senate)	1984	$72,600 per year
1796-1815	$6 per diem	1985-1986	$75,100 per year
1815-1817	$1,500 per year	January 1987	$77,400 per year
1817-1855	$8 per diem	March 1987-1989	$89,500 per year
1855-1865	$3,000 per year	1990	$96,600 per year (House)
1865-1871	$5,000 per year	1990	$98,400 per year (Senate)
1871-1873	$7,500 per year	January 1991-	$125,100 per year (House)
1873-1907	$5,000 per year		$101,900 per year (Senate)
1907-1925	$7,500 per year	August 1991-	$125,100 per year (Senate)
1925-1932	$10,000 per year		
1932-1933	$9,000 per year		
1933-1935	$8,500 per year		
1935-1947	$10,000 per year		
1947-1955	$12,500 per year		
1955-1965	$22,500 per year		
1965-1969	$30,000 per year		
1969-1975	$42,500 per year		
1975-1977	$44,600 per year		
1977-1979	$57,500 per year		
1979-82	$60,662.50 per year*		

* Percentage increases in congressional salaries generally are rounded to the nearest $100. The 1979 increase was not rounded because of specific language in the enacting legislation.

Note: The top six leaders of Congress—the Speaker of the House, the Senate president pro tempore, and the majority and minority leaders of both chambers—receive additional pay. Highest paid is the House Speaker, who earned $160,600 in 1991.

Sources: Congressional Research Service; House Sergeant at Arms; Senate Disbursing Office.

prevent a pay hike for members of Congress.

Lawmakers automatically got a 3.5 percent pay increase as of January 1, 1984, under the 1975 comparability pay law that gave members of Congress the same cost-of-living raises as federal workers. (President Reagan had recommended the increase in 1983 but had delayed its effective date from October 1, 1983, to January 1, 1984.)

In April Congress raised its pay another one-half percent in the 1983 Budget Reconciliation Act. The raise was retroactive to January.

The actual increase in take-home pay in 1984 amounted to less than $270, however, because lawmakers began paying Social Security taxes that

year. Until 1984 members of Congress, like federal workers, were not covered by the Social Security system and instead received pension benefits from a separate retirement plan. But to keep the Social Security system solvent, Congress cleared legislation in 1983 that required members of Congress and all federal workers to join the system.

Senate Objections. Because Congress did not have to vote on the 3.5 percent pay increase, several Senate Republicans objected to what they called the "backdoor" pay hike.

In January the Senate took up a bill by Don Nickles, R-Okla., that would have rescinded the

3.5 percent increase for members of Congress but not other federal employees. During debate on the measure, Nickles said, "The country is going broke with deficits. It is hard for those of us who like to see cuts in every area, including defense, to accept a raise."

"If Congress wants a pay raise, they ought to be willing to have it up on the floor for everyone to see and vote up or down," said Jake Garn, R-Utah, a cosponsor of the bill. "We have had sneaky ones over the years, but this is the worst one."

Opponents of the bill argued that the salary rollback—which would have saved about $1.3 million in 1984—was a feeble gesture at budget austerity in the face of $200 billion budget deficits.

"If we really want to get down to the core, we will get into the areas where we are really spending money," said Barry Goldwater, R-Ariz. "Take a look at the welfare state."

Others warned that if salaries were not adequate to cover the high cost of maintaining homes both in their states and in Washington, members would be forced to rely more heavily on honoraria and other outside earnings.

Even Nickles, who said he would be "disappointed" if the House did not pass the measure, conceded that most senators would be relieved if the bill died in the House, which is what happened.

On January 26, senators voted 66-19 to revoke the $2,400 comparability increase. But the bill never made it to the House floor.

House leaders from both parties wanted to protect members from a politically risky vote during an election year. "I would think it is extraordinarily unwise for us to follow the action of the Senate and interrupt the cost-of-living adjustment," said Majority Whip Thomas S. Foley, D-Wash.

By referring the measure to the House Post Office and Civil Service Committee, whose chairman, William D. Ford, D-Mich., was known to favor regular pay increases, leaders ensured the bill's demise.

Second Raise.   Congress got another slight salary increase when the Senate on April 5 cleared, 67-26, a budget reconciliation bill left over from 1983. Several senators were unhappy about the half percent increase in congressional pay included in the House-passed measure. But Senate Budget Committee Chairman Pete V. Domenici, R-N.M., said he did not want to change the House version and jeopardize the other savings that would be achieved under the legislation.

1985-1986: Pay Freeze

Members of Congress again got a 3.5 percent comparability increase on January 1, 1985, along with their staffs and federal workers. The pay hike boosted congressional salaries to $75,100 a year. The raise, which had been proposed by President Reagan in August 1984 for federal employees, applied to members of Congress under a 1975 law. (Like the previous comparability increase this one had been scheduled to take effect October 1, 1984, but was delayed until January 1, 1985.)

The Commission on Executive, Legislative, and Judicial Salaries, which met every four years to recommend major adjustments in pay for top federal officials, did not recommend a congressional salary increase in 1985. Instead, it called for procedural changes in the way Congress rejected the president's recommendation for a pay raise and also proposed that another commission then convene in 1986 to recommend salary changes.

In August the president recommended a pay freeze rather than a comparability raise for federal employees for 1986. Congress included a freeze on its own salaries in a budget reconciliation bill, which cleared March 20, 1986.

1987: Reagan Plan

The next increase in congressional pay came in 1987, when members' salaries jumped from $75,100 to $89,500. Lawmakers first got a 3 percent comparability raise on January 1 along with federal employees. The pay hike was included in a catchall fiscal 1987 appropriations bill passed in 1986.

In February members accepted a $12,100 increase that had been proposed by President Reagan based on the study of the specially convened Commission on Executive, Legislative, and Judicial Salaries.

The commission had proposed a 75 percent increase for lawmakers and argued that the purchasing power of a congressional salary, badly eroded by inflation, had dropped 40 percent since 1969. Instead, Reagan recommended a 16 percent hike.

On January 29, the Senate passed, 88-6, a measure to reject the proposed raise, after members said it was wrong for Congress to pay itself more while the government was running record deficits. "Social Security recipients were given a 1.3 percent increase last year," said Strom Thurmond, R-S.C., who sponsored the resolution to block the increase. "Yet we consider giving ourselves a 16 percent increase. There is no rational justification for such action."

Senators then added an amendment blocking the pay raise to a House-passed bill to aid the homeless. The move infuriated House Democrats, who had made homeless aid a top priority. The Senate action also underscored institutional rivalries. House members felt that senators, many of whom were wealthy to begin with, were also more in demand for appearances before special interest groups and thus able to raise more in honoraria than House lawmakers. They said senators were denying them a chance to earn enough to support their families and two homes, in Washington and their districts. "Their position is you have to be a millionaire to be in Congress, or else they're for special interests having control," said Rep. Mike Lowry, D-Wash.

But maneuvering by House Democratic leaders enabled members to go on record against the proposed raise and still pocket the increase. House Speaker Jim Wright, D-Texas, made sure that the House vote on the pay raise came after the thirty-day deadline for disapproving pay proposals under the law. On February 4, the House cleared the homeless aid measure, including the provision rejecting the pay raise, but the action came one day after the deadline.

President Reagan declared the raise in effect. Opponents, who included six members of Congress led by Sen. Gordon J. Humphrey, R-N.H., went to court to repeal the increase, arguing that the raise was enacted unconstitutionally. On June 30, a U.S. district court judge dismissed the lawsuit.

In August Reagan recommended a 2 percent pay hike for federal workers and lawmakers. But Congress denied itself the increase in a fiscal 1988 catchall spending bill that cleared on December 22, 1987.

1989-1990: House Pay Raise

After a storm of public criticism, Congress rejected a 51 percent pay raise in February 1989. Nine months later members approved a hike of almost 40 percent over two years for representatives and top federal officials and more than 10 percent for senators, while tightening ethics rules and limiting outside income.

As a result, House salaries rose to $96,600 in 1990 and $125,100 in 1991. Senators earned $98,400 in 1990 and were to receive $101,900 in 1991.

The measure, which cleared November 18, eliminated a loophole in a 1979 law that had allowed House members who had been in office at the beginning of 1980 to convert campaign funds to personal use once they retired. The legislation also limited expense-paid travel for nongovernmental trips and tightened rules on gifts.

By tying the pay raise to ethics reforms, congressional leaders sought to make the measure more palatable to critics. House Speaker Thomas Foley insisted on calling the measure an "ethics bill," correcting reporters who referred to it as a pay raise.

In the end it was the bipartisanship support of the leadership that pushed the bill through.

The legislation also changed the system for raising congressional pay. In place of the Commission on Executive, Legislative, and Judicial Salaries, the bill established an eleven-member Citizens' Commission on Public Service and Compensation, which was required to meet every four years and report to the president by December 15. The president's pay recommendations, made after receiving the commission's report, would take effect after the next congressional election and only if both the House and the Senate adopted a resolution of approval by recorded vote within sixty days.

The method for providing annual comparability increases was also revised to eliminate the president's role in recommending them. Instead, the congressional comparability raise was automatic and based on private sector wage increases.

Background. On December 13, 1988, the Commission on Executive, Legislative, and Judicial Salaries recommended that members of Congress get a 51 percent pay raise if they agreed to ban honoraria. That would have brought congressional salaries to $135,000, a $45,500 increase.

Members of the commisssion said that a 51 percent pay raise was necessary to make up for two decades of inflation and to provide incentive for members to wean themselves of honoraria.

The higher pay level would have been more

than enough to make up for the loss of honoraria income, even for those who collected the maximum allowed under the law. But because the majority of Americans understood little about honoraria, a promise to give up these speaking fees in exchange for a pay raise failed to provide political cover.

"The honoraria ban never caught on with the public," said former Rep. William R. Ratchford, D-Conn., a member of the commission. "They can relate to a dollar figure on salary, but outside the Beltway, they're not sure what honorarium is."

President Reagan endorsed the 51 percent hike on January 9, which meant that unless Congress passed legislation blocking the increase within thirty days, the raise would take effect.

Advocates of the raise said that continued erosion of congressional salaries would turn lawmaking into a profession only the wealthy could afford. They emphasized that members faced unusually high living costs, including maintaining two residences, one back home and another in Washington.

Fazio, a leading pay-raise advocate, told his colleagues that even if they personally were comfortable living on the salary at that time, they should not block a raise for members from more expensive parts of the country. If their constituents did not think the raise was justified, Fazio said, members did not have to accept the extra money.

"If you can't justify it in South Dakota, don't tell someone who lives in the suburbs of San Francisco to live by the same standard," Fazio said.

But editorial writers slammed Congress not only for the size of the raise but for attempting to avoid a vote on the issue. Congressional offices were flooded with mail from angry constituents.

Some of the harshest criticism came from consumer activist Ralph Nader and a network of radio talk-show hosts around the country who gave people a forum for venting their outrage against the raise. One radio station urged its listeners to send tea bags to congressmen with the slogan, "Read my lips: No pay raise," and thousands did.

Members of Congress started going public against the pay raise, even though, in many cases, they were privately hoping to get the money.

The Senate voted 95-5 on February 2, 1989, to disapprove of the proposed raise for members of Congress and senior officials in the executive and legislative branches. The vote increased pressure on the House.

House Speaker Wright, who had promised to keep pay raise legislation off the House floor, was forced to reverse his position when a majority of members voted for consideration of the matter.

During debate on the raise, Ways and Means Chairman Dan Rostenkowski, D-Ill., gave an emotional defense of the raise. "I can't remember a more disheartening or embarrassing debate," he said. "I am proud of what I do and you, my colleagues, should feel the same way."

But after the outpouring of criticism, few were willing to test their worth at the voting booth.

On February 7, one day before the raise was to take effect, the House voted 380-48 to kill the pay raise for all three branches. The Senate quickly followed suit, 94-6.

Round Two. As soon as he became Speaker June 6, Foley urged a bipartisan task force that had been named by Wright to look at ethics laws to report quickly. It was understood that the centerpiece of that effort, eliminating honoraria payments, could only fly if members' lost income was offset by a salary increase.

The task force, headed by Fazio and Lynn Martin, R-Ill., came up with a plan intended to avoid the pitfalls of the previous pay hike effort. The plan called for a two-stage increase and delayed the larger hike until after the next election so voters could decide whether incumbents deserved the raise. And from the beginning, leaders said they would put the proposal to a roll-call vote. Proponents decided to leave it to the Senate to set its own salary and ethics rules.

The ethics-pay raise package came to the House floor on November 16. House Speaker Foley and Minority Leader Robert H. Michel, R-Ill., put the full weight and prestige of their offices behind the pay raise, in a show of bipartisanship missing in the earlier pay-raise drive.

"The Speaker and minority leader were behind this 100 percent—that was the key," said John P. Murtha, D-Pa., a veteran from the front lines of past fights for pay raises.

Few spoke in opposition to the bill. "We told people, if they couldn't be for it, at least don't be a leader of the opposition," said Steve Gunderson of Wisconsin, a deputy GOP whip.

The House approved the measure 252-174.

Senate Action. Senate leaders of both parties presented a united front in support of the two-step pay increase. But despite concerted arm-twisting in the closing hours of the session, they failed to muster the votes for the House package and had to quickly come up with a smaller raise to apply to senators.

When the initial pay-raise proposal appeared to be foundering, Assistant Senate GOP leader Alan K. Simpson of Wyoming called his House counterpart, Minority Whip Newt Gingrich of Georgia, for lobbying help from House members. House members descended onto the Senate floor to buttonhole their colleagues.

Unpersuaded were several Democratic senators with presidential ambitions—Sam Nunn of Georgia, Bill Bradley of New Jersey, and Al Gore of Tennessee—and some of the richest members, including Herb Kohl, D-Wis., and John D. Rockefeller IV, D-W.Va.

The House plan never came to a direct vote in the Senate. After off-the-floor discussions, Senate leaders conceded failure and offered a proposal that left the raise intact for House members and top government officials but raised Senate salaries by 10 percent and provided cost-of-living raises in the future. The vote on the plan was 56-43, with more than three-quarters of those facing reelection voting no.

1991: Pay-Honoraria Tradeoff

As 1991 began, House members were barred from accepting honoraria, and senators, while still able to accept speaking fees, were limited to a smaller overall amount. Between pay and honoraria, senators could earn roughly as much as representatives.

Both chambers got a 3.6 percent comparability increase, and the House received a 25 percent raise as well under the two-tiered system established in 1989.

Comparability Formula. The size of the comparability increase was determined by a formula linking congressional salaries to private sector pay, instead of federal worker increases, as in the past.

The new method for figuring the increase was set in the 1989 law and replaced the procedure for automatic annual increases that had been in effect since 1975. By basing annual congressional pay increases on the Bureau of Labor Statistics' quarterly index of wages and salaries for private industry, lawmakers hoped to ensure annual pay raises for themselves without having to revisit the politically painful issue year after year.

1991 Senate Pay Raise. Before departing for the August congressional recess, the Senate voted to give itself a 23 percent raise to bring senators' annual salaries up to the House level of $125,100.

The Senate made its move when the legislative branch appropriations bill arrived on the floor July 17. Though it was widely known that a pay raise was in the works, the bill was brought up suddenly once Appropriations Committee Chairman Robert C. Byrd, D-W.Va., had the votes in hand. The Senate adopted his amendment, 53-45.

The House agreed to go along, but only after forcing Senate negotiators to ease congressional limits on accepting gifts and to join the House and the rest of the federal government in banning honoraria.

NOTES

1. James Madison, *Notes of Debates in the Federal Convention of 1787* (Athens: Ohio University Press, 1966), 198.

2. Unless otherwise noted, the account of action on congressional pay is drawn from the *Congressional Quarterly Almanac* and *Congressional Quarterly Weekly Report* for various years.

3. Paul E. Dwyer, "Salaries of Members of Congress: Congressional Votes, 1967-1989," Congressional Research Service, March 3, 1989.

CHAPTER 2

Honoraria:

A Vanishing Perquisite

Succumbing to pressure from voters, public interest lobbying groups, and a growing number of members, first the House and then the Senate agreed to give up one of their most cherished perquisites. Beginning in 1991, House members could no longer keep for themselves honoraria—the payment of money or anything of value an organization makes to a legislator in return for a speech, appearance, or article. The Senate approved the honoraria ban in mid-1991, as part of the annual legislative branch appropriations bill. The ban took effect upon enactment of the bill, but senators were permitted to keep speaking fees received earlier in 1991 (up to the $23,068 limit that previously had been set for the year).

"I think it's the end of honoraria," Sen. Howard M. Metzenbaum, D-Ohio, said after the Senate voted in favor of the ban in July 1991. "We're never going to go back to that," added Assistant Republican Leader Alan K. Simpson, Wyo.[1]

Always reluctant to raise their own salaries for fear of the political repercussions that inevitably followed, members of Congress had long viewed the acceptance of honoraria as a supplement to their regular pay. As inflation eroded congressional salaries, honoraria became an even more important source of income for many legislators of modest means.

Honoraria were also a time-honored way for private organizations and associations to get an "insider's view" of Washington. Most of the honoraria members earned came from speeches to conventions held by trade associations, other business groups, and labor unions. Education groups, schools and colleges, foreign policy associations, religious, ethnic, and civic groups, and so-called single issue organizations (such as pro- and anti-abortion groups) that often have an ideological bias also paid legislators in exchange for a briefing or speech.

Honoraria also were used by corporate boards of directors or small groups of business executives, lawyers, lobbyists, and others for intimate meetings with members of Congress, perhaps over breakfast or lunch. These groups said a meal and a chat with a prominent senator or representative was worth the $1,000 or $2,000 payment because of the opportunity it provided for an off-the-record exchange of views. For many smaller interest groups that could not afford campaign contributions on the same scale as bigger organizations, honoraria were particularly valuable in reaching lawmakers.

R. Michael Jenkins

Sen. Robert C. Byrd, D-W.Va., almost single-handedly delivered the votes in 1991 for a pay increase/honoraria ban. Said Byrd: "There is nothing honorable about honoraria. It is simply a way for special interests to gain access to senators. . . ."

Organizations that gave honoraria—and members of Congress who accepted them—denied any impropriety. Many freely admitted, however, that inviting a member to address an organization's annual convention or meet with executives—and paying him or her for the appearance—could have important benefits. Top management at the organization gained a better understanding of the Washington scene and got an expert assessment of the chances for passage of legislation of interest to the organization. Such meetings also provided an occasion to get to know an important member, to apprise him of the organization's views, and to ensure easier access to the member in the future. These meetings also could be used to let the member know he had the support of influential groups in his state or congressional district.

In the opinion of many, however, paying legislators for speeches or appearances smacked of legalized bribery. Like campaign funds, the payment of honoraria could be construed as a means to ensure that a legislator would, at the least, give special consideration to the viewpoint of the organization making the payment. When a member accepts a $2,000 honorarium from an industry group, said Rep. Tom Harkin, D-Iowa in 1981, "he's going to tell them what they want to hear." [2]

In the mid-1970s critics of the practice succeeded in placing limits on the amount of honoraria that a lawmaker could collect for any one speech or appearance or keep in any one year (any amount taken in over the total had to be donated to charity). Despite those restrictions, the total amount of honoraria paid to members of Congress increased steadily. In 1989 lawmakers collected more than $9 million overall in honoraria, compared with a total of $2.7 million just ten years earlier. The amount of honoraria declined in 1990, totaling $7.7 million. [3]

Movements to place tighter restrictions on honoraria or to ban them altogether faltered in the early and mid-1980s. Members acknowledged their growing political vulnerability to charges of impropriety. "I personally always got all the honoraria I could," said Rep. Charles Wilson, D-Texas, in 1987. "But in the future it could be a bad campaign issue." [4] At least twenty senators and 110 representatives reported that they received no honoraria in 1989, while at least two senators and twenty-two House members donated all of their honoraria earnings to charity. Many other members did not keep the full amount allowed under the rules.

Nonetheless, many lawmakers were unwilling to give up honoraria without a compensatory pay increase. But the public outcry that arose whenever the question of raising congressional pay came up made members reluctant to act on either front.

A breakthrough came in late 1989, when the House agreed to accept a substantial pay raise in return for a ban on honoraria. The decision might have been driven more by political expediency than ethical imperatives. During the 1988 election campaigns, challengers had needled several incumbents about their acceptance of honoraria. Criticisms that Sen. Lowell P. Weicker, Jr., was making speeches for pay when he should have been voting in the Senate helped Democrat Joseph I. Lieberman unseat the veteran Republican from Connecticut. At the same time Speaker Jim Wright, D-Texas, was defending himself, unsuccessfully, against several charges of impropriety, including one that he had engaged in a scheme to avoid the House limits on honoraria.

Even more reluctant than the House to abandon honoraria, the Senate in 1989 settled for a smaller pay increase and a system for phasing down the amount of honoraria each senator could legally accept. But pressure continued in the Senate, and in July 1991 the Senate finally voted to raise its salary to the same level as the House and to bar senators from pocketing any honoraria. Like House members, senators must donate any fees they receive for speeches, appearances, or articles to charity.

INITIAL LIMITATIONS ON HONORARIA

Until 1975 there were no restrictions on such earnings, and it was not unusual for prominent members of Congress to earn more from honoraria than from their salary.

The era of completely unregulated honoraria payments ended on January 1, 1975, when Congress's first campaign finance law took effect. That measure limited honoraria payments to members and other federal officials to $1,000 for a single speaking engagement or article and set a cap of $15,000 a year on total honoraria that a member could keep. The restrictions had an effect: eighty-one senators reported earning $637,893 in 1975, down more than $300,000 from the previous year. (House members were not required to report honoraria until 1978.)

The restrictions were loosened considerably by provisions of the Federal Election Campaign Act Amendments of 1976. That law raised the ceiling on payments for a single speech or article to $2,000 and raised the annual amount permitted to $25,000. The $25,000 was a net amount and did not include booking agents' fees, travel expenditures, subsistence, and expenses for an aide or a spouse accompanying the lawmaker.

The 1976 law permitted members to deduct any funds donated to charity or used to pay out-of-pocket expenses from their total yearly honoraria earnings for the purpose of complying with the $25,000 limitation.

In addition, under the 1976 law House and Senate members could receive honoraria earned in previous years without applying those payments to their current year's limit. In 1977, the first year in which the campaign act amendments were in effect, eighty-one senators earned almost $1.1 million.

ETHICS CODES LIMITS

The House and Senate further limited the amount of honoraria lawmakers could accept when both chambers passed new ethics codes in 1977. As of January 1, 1979, no member of either the House or the Senate could accept more than 15 percent of his or her annual salary in outside earned income, including honoraria. The House further limited the honorarium a representative could accept for a single speech, appearance, or article to $750; the Senate limit was set at $1,000. (The House limit was raised to $1,000 in January 1979, the first month the limitations were in effect.)

The codes did not affect unearned income, such as dividends, interest payments, or rent from properties. The codes also exempted from the limitations income members earned from family farms and small businesses.

In both chambers the limits on outside earned

incomes were the most controversial provisions of the ethics codes. House Speaker Thomas P. O'Neill, Jr., D-Mass., and Senate Majority Leader Robert C. Byrd, D-W.Va., made passage of a strong ethics code a condition for approval of salary increases for Congress and top executive officials, which the two men believed were sorely needed. Both leaders said that a limit on outside income was essential to a strong code. O'Neill called the provision "the heart and soul of the entire package" of ethical standards.

Nonetheless, members in both chambers tried to strike the provisions from the two codes. Their principal argument was that the limitations would discriminate in favor of wealthy lawmakers. The restrictions, argued Rep. Otis G. Pike, D-N.Y., would "create a Congress of two kinds of people. Some will have large unearned incomes and the rest will need their political jobs in order to feed and clothe and educate their families. Whether this will be a more ethical Congress only time will tell, but I think not."

But backers of the limit on earned income argued that it was necessary to cut down the large amounts of money that special interest groups could contribute to members. "I believe that there is a real potential for conflict of interest when a senator takes large sums of money for speaking to groups who have a direct interest in legislation before this body," said Sen. Dick Clark, D-Iowa.[5]

The leaders prevailed in the end. The House rejected a move to delete the limitations on earned income, 79-344; the Senate defeated a similar amendment, 35-62.

SENATE DELAY

The Senate limitation was never implemented. In March 1979, the year the cap was to take effect,

Teresa Zabala

Sen. David L. Boren addresses the American Association of Retired Persons. Until the practice was banned in 1991, many members of Congress supplemented their incomes with speaking fees from private interests, known as honoraria.

the Senate voted to delay implementation of those requirements until 1983. The delay had the effect of leaving a senator's maximum honorarium payment at $2,000 and annual honoraria earnings at $25,000—the ceilings set in the 1976 campaign finance law.

Senators were being paid $57,500 at the beginning of 1979, and the 15 percent limitation on total honoraria would have allowed them to earn another $8,625. Financial disclosure figures for 1978 showed that fifty-nine senators in office in 1979 had earned more than that in honoraria and would likely have suffered a reduction in their total income if the delay had not been approved. Instead, eighty-six senators received total honoraria payments of $1.2 million in 1979, an average of nearly $14,000 for each member who accepted honoraria.

Senate action on the delay came on short notice and passed by voice vote with only a handful of members on the floor. Although some senators complained about the way the delay was handled, the Senate three weeks later rejected an attempt to overturn the delay, 44-54.

ANNUAL LIMITS LIFTED

In October 1981 the Senate repealed the $25,000 limit on outside earned income imposed by the 1976 campaign finance act (although it left the $2,000 limit on the amount a senator could accept for a single speech or article). Sen. Ted Stevens, R-Alaska, argued that since senators had an unlimited income from other sources they should be entitled to unlimited payments from speeches. Although the change came late in 1981, twenty-five senators still earned more than $25,000 in honoraria that year. Several senators, however, continued to give all or part of their honoraria to charity.

After the Senate removed its annual honoraria limit, representatives complained that they deserved equal treatment. In a surprise move, the House leadership on December 15, 1981, brought to the floor a change in House rules that would double House members' allowable outside earnings, from 15 percent to 30 percent of their official salary. The change was approved unanimously in less than half a minute. Only a handful of members were present.

At an annual salary of $60,662.50, House members could earn up to $18,198.75 a year in honoraria, beginning in 1981. That compared to a ceiling of $9,099.37 under the lower limit. Since the ceiling was lifted so late in the year, members had only about two weeks to earn the additional income. Despite the deadline, more than seventy representatives reported outside income in excess of $9,100 for 1981.

The Senate's 1981 action eliminated the limits on accepting honoraria for 1981 and 1982. But the 15 percent cap on outside earnings contained in the Senate Ethics Code was still scheduled to take effect in 1983. In December 1982 the Senate repealed that cap; the only restriction on honoraria continued to be the $2,000 maximum for each appearance or speech. In return for lifting the cap, the Senate agreed to forgo a 15 percent pay increase that the House had voted itself.

ANNUAL LIMIT IMPOSED IN SENATE

The pay and honoraria differentials between the two chambers were short-lived. In May 1983 congressional financial disclosure statements were released showing that more than half of the senators earned honoraria totaling more than 30 percent of their salaries.

Pressured by the public and the House, the Senate in 1983 agreed to put a 30 percent limit on the total amount of honoraria a member could accept in a single year in exchange for a pay raise. The controversial measure was passed by a vote of

49-47. Senate action meant that both chambers were again paid the same amount, $69,800, and that legislators could accept no more than $20,940 in honoraria.

Two years later the Senate raised the cap on honoraria and other outside earned income to 40 percent of a senator's official salary. Early in 1986, by voice vote and with few members on the floor, the House also raised its cap to 40 percent. The following day, the House reversed that vote, leaving the cap at 30 percent.

HONORARIA BARRED IN HOUSE

Neither chamber dealt with the question of honoraria again until 1988, when the Commission on Executive, Legislative, and Judicial Salaries voted in December to recommend a 51 percent pay increase and a ban on honoraria. Members of the commission said that salaries had to be hiked that much to compensate for two decades of inflation—and to provide incentive for the Senate as well as the House to abandon the honoraria system.

From the moment it was announced, however, the pay boost drew criticism. Members quickly discovered that constituents knew little about honoraria, and that a ban gave them little political cover from the outrage the public was expressing about the proposed pay hike. "As far as I can tell, the only people you get money from are the rich," one House member reported a constituent as saying, "and if the rich are so bored, and have nothing better to do, let 'em pay it." [6] In an embarrassing defeat for House Speaker Jim Wright, the House finally voted down the pay raise. (Details, p. 15)

Despite the defeat, pressure continued both for a pay increase and for stronger ethics rules, including a ban on honoraria. The resignations of Speaker Wright and Democratic Whip Tony Coelho, Calif., following allegations that they had violated House rules, made House members particularly eager to find ways to improve Congress's image with the voters. It was clear that a ban on honoraria was likely to be at the heart of any ethics reform.

The plan developed by a bipartisan House task force would raise congressional pay by a third over two years and at the same time overhaul ethics rules and ban honoraria payments. It called for a 7.9 percent increase for legislators and for top executive and judicial branch officials in 1990, to be followed by a 25 percent increase, plus a cost-of-living adjustment, in 1991.

The details of the plan were a closely held secret until the week it was to go to the floor. House Speaker Foley and Republican Leader Michel of Illinois insisted on strong presidential support and did not go public with the task force recommendations until they had a letter of endorsement from President George Bush. In their final drive for rank-and-file backing, members of the Democratic leadership attended a GOP party caucus to drum up support for the package; Republican leaders, including Wright's nemesis, Newt Gingrich of Georgia, attended the caucus.

The resulting discipline was evident when the bill went to the floor on November 16. Few spoke in opposition to the bill, and rhetoric was muted.

The House approved the package, 252-174. Under the terms of the bill, House members, their staff, and other federal officials could not accept honoraria after January 1, 1991, but they could request that charitable contributions be made in their name. Such contributions could not exceed $2,000 and could not be made to any organization that benefited the legislator or his relatives. Federal employees quickly moved to repeal the ban on honoraria that applied to them.

BAN ACCEPTED IN SENATE

As in the House, Senate leaders of both parties presented a united front on the pay raise-honoraria ban, and at first momentum seemed to be in favor of the House package. Senators met in an unusual two-party caucus to plan strategy, and in an early test the Senate voted overwhelmingly to invoke cloture on the bill. But a nose count showed that the leadership was four or five votes short of winning, even after several House members came over to lobby their Senate colleagues.

As a result the House plan never came to a direct vote in the Senate. After several hours of off-the-floor discussions, Senate leaders conceded failure and offered an amendment that left the House salary structure intact, along with the executive and judicial branch salaries, but raised Senate salaries by only 10 percent and provided future cost-of-living raises. Instead of banning them outright, the Senate bill reduced the ceiling on honoraria that senators could keep from 40 percent of salary in 1989 to 27 percent in 1990—$26,568 for most senators. (Senate leaders earned slightly higher salaries than rank-and-file members and therefore could retain slightly more in honoraria.) Any cost-of-living pay increase implemented after December 31, 1990, was to be accompanied by an equivalent reduction in the ceiling on honoraria until it reached zero. The Senate approved that amendment, 56-43, and the House cleared the bill by accepting the Senate changes.

In August 1990 the Senate for the first time voted to ban honoraria, but the amendment, offered by Christopher J. Dodd, D-Conn., was attached to a controversial campaign finance bill that died in conference. Dodd offered his amendment to another campaign finance bill in May 1991, and again the Senate passed it by a wide margin. But again passage of the campaign finance bill was in doubt; President Bush had threatened to veto the bill. "In fact," said Republican Leader Bob Dole, Kan., "many of my colleagues are counting on the president's veto as a way to vote 'yes' on the honoraria ban today while taking honoraria tomorrow." [7]

The House ban left the Senate in the embarrassing position of being the only part of the federal government where acceptance of honoraria was not illegal. Senators took in nearly $2 million in honoraria in 1990, down about $700,000 from the previous year. At least twenty-seven senators accepted no honoraria in 1990, and another five gave all their honoraria to charity. Senators were also piqued that their salaries were not only less than the amount that House members received but also less than what several House staffers earned.

When the fiscal 1992 legislative appropriations bill came to the Senate floor on July 17, Appropriations Committee Chairman Robert Byrd, backed by the Democratic and Republican leaders, offered an amendment to raise senators' pay 25 percent in exchange for a ban on honoraria. The pay hike would mean that senators and representatives once again earned the same amounts. The amendment was approved, 53-45.

Even though both houses had apparently closed the door on keeping honoraria, a loophole remained open. Besides the fee, members (and frequently their wives) often receive expense-paid trips to the sites where the speeches are given, as well as lodging and meals. In 1989 both chambers curbed the length of the trips that members could accept from private organizations but set no limits on the amounts of expenses that members could accept. *(Box, p. 39)*

NOTES

1. Janet Hook, "Senate's Ban on Honoraria Marks End of an Era," *Congressional Quarterly Weekly Report,* July 22, 1991, 1955.

2. *Congressional Quarterly Almanac 1981* (Washington, D.C.: Congressional Quarterly, 1982), 287.

3. "Members' 1989 Honoraria Receipts," *Congressional Quarterly Weekly Report,* June 2, 1990, 1749-1753; "Members' 1990 Honoraria Receipts," *Congres-*

sional Quarterly Weekly Report, June 22, 1991, 1694-1698.

4. Janet Hook, "Proposal for 51 Percent Pay Hike Sets Up Fracas," *Congressional Quarterly Weekly Report,* December 17, 1988, 3527.

5. *Congressional Quarterly Almanac 1977* (Washington, D.C.: Congressional Quarterly, 1978), 768, 773.

6. Beth Donovan, "Parties Find Ethics Tough Sell as Local Campaign Issue," *Congressional Quarterly Weekly Report,* July 15, 1989, 1813.

7. Phil Kuntz, "Honoraria Ban Still Just an Idea," *Congressional Quarterly Weekly Report,* May 25, 1991, 1353.

CHAPTER 3

The Franking Privilege:

A Potent Perquisite

From the day newly elected members arrive in Washington to the day they leave Congress, lawmakers are presented with an array of allowances and benefits that help to ease the pressures of congressional life.

Members of Congress enjoy free mailing privileges for official business and use of free office space in federal buildings in their home states or districts. Each member receives, in addition to salary, an official expense allowance for travel, telephone and telegraph services, stationery, postage and newsletters, and office expenses and equipment. *(Congressional salaries, p. 1)*

Members are allowed free storage of files and records, free office decorations, use of television and radio recording studios at less than commercial rates, authority to make certain patronage appointments, discounts at Capitol Hill shops, free or low-cost services, and hundreds of free publications. They also can receive various health protection plans and free emergency care while at work, life insurance, and a generous retirement pension.

Senators and representatives have access to elaborate computerized mailing and legislative analysis systems and to the latest recreation facilities—swimming pools, saunas, masseurs, and gymnasiums. Legislative counsels, legal counsels, chaplains, photographers, and Internal Revenue Service advisers stand by at the Capitol to assist members. Attractive dining rooms, barber and beauty shops, and convenient rail and airline ticket offices are available in the Capitol and congressional office buildings.

Trying to calculate the total amount of money Congress spends on itself can be very difficult. Some information is readily available in the semiannual reports of the secretary of the Senate and quarterly reports of the clerk of the House. These publications list the salaries for all congressional employees and many expenditures made by members in their official duties. But it is hard to attach a dollar value to many fringe benefits. *(Cost of major allowances, box, p. 46)*

The Tax Foundation, a Washington-based research organization, estimated in 1991 that each senator cost the taxpayer $4.6 million annually and each representative cost $1.6 million. The Tax Foundation also estimated that the cost of Congress had more than doubled since 1980 and was more than seven times higher than in 1970.

Legislative branch appropriations, which included funding for Congress itself and for several

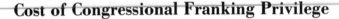

Cost of Congressional Franking Privilege

(in millions)

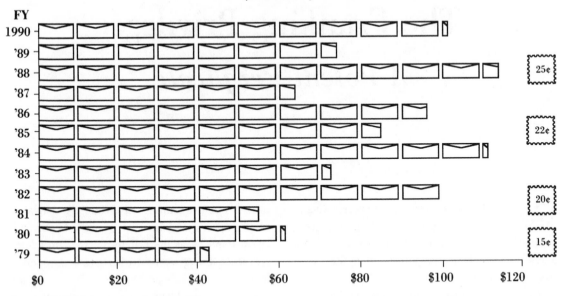

Source: Clerk of the House; U.S. Postal Service.

related agencies, such as the Library of Congress, came to $2.2 billion in fiscal 1991. *(Fiscal 1991 appropriations, box, p. 54)*

GUIDELINES ON FRANKING

The franking privilege is one of the most valuable and controversial of members' perquisites of office. Every year millions of American households receive pieces of mail that bear a facsimile of the signature of a member of Congress, known as the frank, in place of a stamp. Mailing letters and packages under one's signature at taxpayers' expense is one of the nation's oldest privileges—the Continental Congress adopted the practice in 1775.

Through newsletters and other mailings, sent at government expense, legislators can communicate directly with their constituents, informing them about congressional decisions and passing on useful news about the federal government.

The franked envelope might contain a legislator's response to a constituent question or request, a copy of his newsletter, a survey, a press release, a packet of voting information, government publications or reports, or other printed matter that in some way relates to the legislator's "official duties."

Mailings related to political campaigns or political parties, personal business, or friendships may not be franked. A lawmaker, for example, cannot use the frank on a holiday greeting, a message of sympathy, an invitation to a party fundraiser, or a request for political support. Nonetheless, opponents of the frank argue that it gives incumbents running for reelection a great boost over challengers who do not have the same cheap access to the voters.

Although no stamp is needed, a franked letter is not actually mailed free of charge. Each year, as part of the legislative appropriations bill, Congress appropriates a certain amount of money to cover the cost of members' franking.

The U.S. Postal Service keeps records on how many franked pieces of mail it handles and how much they weigh and periodically sends Congress what amounts to a bill. If Congress has not appropriated enough money to cover the costs of franked mail, it does so in a supplemental appropriations bill.

The Postal Service, however, is obligated to send all franked mail whether or not Congress appropriates enough money to cover the costs.

COSTS AND CONTROVERSIES

Cost is one of the most criticized aspects of the franking privilege. The cost of franked mail jumped dramatically in the 1970s and 1980s because of increases in both mailing rates and the amount of mail legislators sent under the frank. Mailing costs increased more than fourfold from 1972 to 1988; even adjusted for inflation, that represented an 86 percent increase.

An even more controversial issue, however, has been the advantage that the franking privilege gives incumbents over challengers. Despite restrictions on political content and self-promotion, members can and do take advantage of loopholes and lax regulation. For example, although members are cautioned against mass mailings of *Congressional Record* reprints containing statements of praise by another member, the mailings may be prefaced by a colleague's comments on the member's insightful analysis. Members' newsletters regularly report awards presented to the law-

maker as well as favorable ratings of his or her voting record by various interest groups. Although members are cautioned about the overuse of the word "I" and their name and photograph in franked material, there is little enforcement of the guidelines.

As the use of computerized mailings has grown more sophisticated, members increasingly have used the frank to target mass mailings, telling a selected group of people what they want to hear and, probably just as important, avoiding arousing groups thought to be unsympathetic. A lawmaker, for example, may tell farmers of his support for wheat exports, teachers of his support for education, small businesses of his opposition to an increase in the minimum wage.

Despite restrictions on use of the frank during the sixty days preceding primary and general elections, the amount spent on the frank has invariably gone up in election years. Between 1976 and 1988 mail volume in election years averaged 51.4 percent more than in preceding years. In 1987-88 the Senate spent $53 million on franked mail; more than $20 million of that total was spent by the twenty-seven senators running for reelection in 1988, according to Common Cause, the citizens' lobbying group that has long opposed use of the frank. "The frank is being used as a campaign subsidy—unabashedly and outrageously," said Sen. Gordon Humphrey, R-N.H.[1]

By the late 1980s Congress was forced to deal with the way it used the frank, just as it had been forced to reexamine its use of other perquisites. The results of that examination were new rules in each chamber that allotted each member a specific mail budget and required each to disclose publicly the amount spent on franked mail. Individual disclosure was expected to slow increases in the cost of franked mail, perhaps even to reduce it. But critics continued to argue that even with the new limitations, the frank still gave members an unfair political advantage.

FRANKING REGULATIONS

Under the regulations dealing with the franking privilege (Title 39, Section 3210, of the U.S. Code), persons authorized to use the frank include the vice president, members and members-elect of Congress (senators, representatives, delegates, and resident commissioners), and officers of the House and Senate.

In addition, the surviving spouse of a member who dies is permitted to use the frank for nonpolitical correspondence related to the death of the member. The authorization expires 180 days after the member's death.

Members and others vested with the franking privilege are entitled, on a restricted basis, to use the frank during the ninety days immediately following the date on which they leave office. During this period use of the frank is limited to matters directly related to the closing of the member's congressional office. Former members may not send newsletters, questionnaires, or other mass-mailed material.

Standing, select, special, or joint committees of Congress, as well as subcommittees and commissions, may send mail under the frank of the chairman, the ranking minority member, or any other member of the committee. Exceptions are "informal" or "ad hoc" groups of lawmakers—such as the House Democratic Study Group or the House Wednesday Group of Republicans—whose business relates to political, party policy, or special interest matters.

The franking regulations prohibit a person entitled to use the frank from lending it to any nonmember, private committee, organization, or association. Use of the frank for the benefit of charitable organizations, political action committees, trade organizations, and other groups is expressly forbidden. In addition, the frank may not be used for mail that is to be delivered to a foreign country.

What May Be Franked

Despite these restrictions, a wide range of material may be sent out under the frank. The law states that the frank is designed to "assist and expedite the conduct of the official business, activities, and duties of the Congress of the United States." The terms "official business and activities" are broadly defined to cover "all matters which directly or indirectly pertain to the legislative process or to any congressional representative functions generally, or to the functioning, working, or operating of the Congress and the performance of official duties in connection therewith, and shall include, *but not be limited to,* the conveying of information to the public, and the requesting of the views of the public, or the views and information of other authority of government, as a guide or a means of assistance in the performance of those functions." (Emphasis added)

Among the major categories of mail eligible for the franking privilege are:

Newsletters and News Releases. The law authorizes use of the congressional frank for "the usual and customary congressional newsletter or press release, which may deal with such matters as the impact of laws and decisions on State and local government and individual citizens; reports on public and official actions taken by Members of Congress; and discussions of proposed or pending legislation of governmental actions and the position of the Members of Congress on, and arguments for or against, such matters."

Examples of frankable material in newsletters or news releases include tabulations of a member's voting record; reports on the lawmaker's position on various legislative proposals; notices that the member will visit his or her district on official business; statements that are critical of administration or congressional policies—provided they are not presented in a partisan manner; invitations to meet and participate with another lawmaker in a public discussion or report on Congress if the meeting is not held under political auspices; and a member's financial disclosure statement.

Questionnaires. Members may mail under the frank "the usual and customary congressional questionnaire seeking public opinion on any law, pending or proposed legislation, public issue, or subject." Members may not permit the frank to be used for the return of responses, but the results of the member's surveys may be included in a newsletter or other form of allowable franked correspondence. A member may not ask the recipient of a questionnaire to indicate whether he or she is a Republican or Democrat.

Mailgrams. Members may also send Mailgrams under the frank, provided the material conforms to the same guidelines used in sending mail under the franking law.

Other Material. Other materials that may be franked include mail to any individual or agency and to officials at any level of government regarding programs and proposed legislation; congressional committee and floor action and other related matters of public concern or public service; mail between members, mail from a member's Capitol Hill office to his congressional district offices (or between district offices), or from a member to a state or local legislator; nonpartisan voter registration or election information or assistance; biographical or autobiographical material of a member or the member's family that is mailed as a part of a federal publication or in response to a specific request and is not intended for publicity purposes; and mail, including general mass mailings, that consists of federal laws or regulations, government publications or publications purchased with federal funds, and publications containing items of general information.

Franking Privilege Upheld

On May 2, 1983, the Supreme Court rejected a challenge to the free mailing privileges accorded members of Congress (authorized persons include the vice president, senators, representatives, delegates, and resident commissioners). Putting an end to a decade-old lawsuit, the Court voted 6-3 not to consider the case. The vote left standing a lower court decision upholding the constitutionality of the congressional franking privilege.

The suit had been brought in 1973 by Common Cause, the public interest lobby, which charged that the frank was unconstitutional because it promoted the reelection of incumbents and therefore placed an unfair disadvantage on challengers. On September 7, 1982, a special three-judge panel of the U.S. District Court for the District of Columbia dismissed the Common Cause suit. The panel said the franking privilege "confers a substantial advantage to incumbent congressional candidates over their challengers" but found no constitutional violation.

Despite its ultimate rejection, the Common Cause suit *(Common Cause v. William F. Bolger)* had a substantial impact on the franking privilege. Between 1973, when the suit was first filed, and 1983, Congress had placed several restrictions on use of the frank meant to limit the most egregious abuses of its use.

The changes did not satisfy Common Cause, which continued to maintain that the frank conferred unfair campaign advantages on incumbents. In its effort to persuade the Supreme Court to hear the case, the lobby group said Congress either should not allow the frank to be used for mass mailings or should also allow nonincumbent challengers to use the frank. In its brief to the Court, Common Cause also suggested that franked mail should not be allowed for mailings to groups of people whose selection identified the mailing as political.

Government publications include, among others, the Department of Agriculture's *Yearbook*, pamphlets and reports, and the *Congressional Record* or a reprint of any part of the *Record*.

The scope of the frank is not limited to these categories, however, and members are advised to seek the opinion of the House Commission on Congressional Mailing Standards or the Senate Ethics and Rules committees, which are authorized to enforce the franking rules and laws.

What May Not Be Franked

In contrast to the broad scope of material that can be franked, the specific prohibitions on use of the frank are defined narrowly. They include "purely personal mailings"; mailings "laudatory and complimentary" of a member "on a purely personal or political basis"; letters consisting solely of condolences to a person who has suffered a loss or congratulations to a person who has achieved some personal distinction (expressions of congratulations to a person who has achieved a public distinction, such as election to public office, graduation from high school, or attainment of U.S. citizenship, may be franked); holiday greetings; reports on how a member spends time other than in connection with his legislative, representative, or "other official functions"; and mailings that "specifically solicit political support."

RESTRICTIONS ON USE

Before 1973 the only standards dealing with the franking privilege were those formulated by the U.S. Postal Service and its predecessor, the U.S. Post Office Department, and by the courts. However, neither postal service actively enforced the regulations, investigating alleged abuses only when private citizens filed official complaints. Conflicting court decisions and the reluctance of many judges to rule on questions of congressional propriety resulted in general confusion about proper use of the frank.

Several disputes about proper use of the frank arose during the 1972 election campaigns. A blatant case of abuse occurred in Georgia, where Rep. Fletcher Thompson, a Republican who was running for the Senate, used the frank to send mail to voters across the state, not just to those in his congressional district. The mailing, which cost taxpayers more than $200,000, became a campaign issue, and a key factor in Thompson's loss to Democrat Sam Nunn. Altogether, twelve cases of abuse reached the courts, helping to convince lawmakers that new regulations were necessary.

1973 Regulations

In 1973 Rep. Morris K. Udall, D-Ariz., introduced a bill establishing specific guidelines for using the franking privilege. The issue, Udall argued, was whether Congress would define the privilege or whether "the judges are going to write the law for us."

The bill, approved by Congress in December 1973, defined the types of mail members could send under the frank, set up mechanisms to rule on individual cases, and restricted the sending of mass mailings (defined as more than five hundred pieces of identical mail) during the four weeks preceding congressional primary and general elections. The law also established in the House a Commission on Congressional Mailing Standards, composed of three Republicans and three Democrats appointed by the Speaker, to resolve franking disputes arising under the law. The Senate Select Committee on Standards and Conduct—later renamed the Select Ethics Committee—was assigned a similar function.

The new regulations, however, did not anticipate every kind of abuse. In 1975 Congress voted to close a loophole in the 1973 law that had allowed former Rep. Frank M. Clark, D-Pa., to send out a franked newsletter to his former constituents two months after his term had expired. The 1975 change permitted former members to use the frank for ninety days after leaving Congress, but only for mailings related to closing down the legislators' offices.

1977 Ethics Code Restrictions

Early in 1977, when new ethics codes were passed, both chambers agreed to additional restrictions on the franking privilege. The House amended its standing rules to impose new limitations on use of the "postal patron" designation—mail that does not specify a recipient's name. The volume of postal patron mail that a member could send annually under the frank was limited to an amount equal to six times the number of addresses in a member's district. All franked postal-patron mailings had to be submitted to the House Commission on Congressional Mailing Standards, which was to advise the member whether the mailing met franking regulations.

In addition, both the House and Senate imposed new regulations on mass mailings—whether sent to a postal-patron address or to a specific person. Mass mailings under the frank were prohibited unless preparation and printing costs were paid entirely from public funds. This restriction was designed to end free political mailings and criticisms that mail printed for a member by special interest groups or political organizations was being sent at government expense. The codes also lengthened the cutoff for sending franked mail before a primary or general election to sixty days.

The Senate included rules in its ethics code that required all franked mass mailings to be registered with the secretary of the Senate. The registration had to include a copy of the material, the number of pieces sent, and a description of the groups receiving the mailing. The information was to be made available for public inspection.

The Senate also provided that its central computer facilities could not be used to store any political or campaign lists and that other mail-related uses of the computer would be subject to guidelines issued by the Senate Ethics Committee.

Changes in the Early 1980s

Sporadically during the 1980s the House and Senate amended their rules and regulations on the frank, sometimes tightening the restrictions, sometimes loosening them. Amendments passed in 1981, for example, gave the Senate Select Ethics Committee and the House Commission on Congressional Mailing Standards statutory authority to enforce the franking rules and laws and to further regulate use of the frank.

The 1981 amendments also allowed senators to make postal-patron mailings, a privilege the House had held since 1973. But in 1982 the Senate Rules and Administration Committee decided to delay implementation of the law after the Senate sergeant at arms reported that if every senator made four such mailings a year, the Senate would have to hire an additional 166 employees and would exceed its mail budget by $57 million. After continued wrangling over the issue, the Rules Committee in November 1983 decided to allow senators to use postal-patron mailings only to announce town meetings.

On the House side, the franking commission in 1983 proposed a new set of rules to blunt criticisms that the frank gave members an unfair political advantage over election challengers. The rules placed limits on the use of photos in newsletters, on the size of the newsletters themselves, and on the size of a member's name in a headline. But after many legislators complained about the proposed restrictions, the commission backed down and issued them as guidelines, rather than rules. "The primary responsibility for ensuring proper and cost-efficient use of the franking privilege," the commission wrote, "lies with each individual member of the House who uses the privilege."

The Senate took a first step toward gaining control of the costs of franked mail in 1986, when it allocated a specific amount of its mail allowance to each senator and required senators to disclose publicly how they had spent their mail allotments. (In 1989 disclosure was shown to be an effective cost-cutter. During the first five months of the year, the Senate spent $6 million on official mail; when disclosure was lifted for the next seven months, spending shot up to $29 million, according to the Senate Rules Committee.)

Individual Budgets, Accountability

Nonetheless, costs continued to mount, as did the criticisms that the frank was an unfair political tool. One limit was imposed in 1989 when both chambers agreed to restrict the mass mailings to three a year, down from six. (Mass mailings notifying constituents of a town meeting or other appearance of the legislator did not count in this limitation, however.)

But the House refused to join the Senate in giving each member a mail budget and making him or her publicly accountable for it. In 1989 the two chambers agreed to set up two separate mail funds, one for the Senate and one for the House. In separate legislation the Senate made part of its permanent rules its procedure for allocating mail funds to members. Ninety percent of the amount allocated to the Senate was to be distributed among senators based on the population of their states. Senators from the largest state, California, received about $1.2 million in fiscal 1990.

The remaining 10 percent was set aside to make sure that no senator received less than $100,000 for mail, to pay for committee mail, and to establish a contingency fund should any senator spend all of his allocation and need more to answer incoming

mail. These rules tended to favor senators from smaller states, because $100,000 was enough to pay for several mailings to every household in small states, while $1.2 million would not cover the cost of even one mailing to every household in California.

The rules still allowed senators to earmark part of their mail money for colleagues, leaving intact a system that let senators up for reelection use mail money from their colleagues who were not facing election. The rules did strike a blow at another cherished Senate perquisite. House members had complained that Senate rules allowed senators to use funds from their campaign accounts to supplement official spending on mass mailings, a practice the House barred. The new rules required any mass mailings to be paid for with appropriated funds.

The Senate also reinstated allocation and disclosure rules that it had suspended for part of the year. Efforts to force House members to adopt similar disclosure rules were unsuccessful in 1989. But in 1990 the House, succumbing to pressure, agreed to give every member a mail budget and require each legislator to disclose the amount spent on franked mail.

The House plan was accepted with great reluctance on the part of many lawmakers. "There is a real concern that we should not retreat" on our use of the frank, said Chief Deputy Whip David E. Bonior, D-Mich., after hearing from colleagues at a meeting of Democratic whips. "Going into a critical campaign in 1992 after redistricting, this is a poor time to start undermining the advantages of incumbency," said another House Democrat. But eventually a majority realized that such restrictions on the frank were "not only necessary but politically inevitable," in the words of Pat Williams, D-Mont.[2]

The restrictions, adopted by voice vote, gave each member an individual mail budget equal to the amount needed to make three first-class mailings to every residential address in the district—about $180,000. Members could supplement their mail budgets by transferring up to $25,000 a year from accounts for other office expenses, but once the budget was depleted, the member had to stop using the frank. Members were required to make quarterly reports on the amount they spent. The House agreed to require that all mailings to more than five hundred recipients be submitted to the House franking commission for approval.

The Senate also tightened its restrictions a bit more in 1990. It barred the transfer of mail funds from one senator to another, and allowed a senator to carry over unused mail funds only to the next fiscal year. Previously, this carryover authority had been unlimited. The Senate also allowed members to transfer money from their mail accounts to other accounts in amounts up to $100,000 or 50 percent of their mass mail budget, whichever was less.

NOTES

1. Weston Kosova, "Congress's Mail Prostitution Ring; Why America Should Be Frank-Incensed," *Washington Monthly,* September 1990, 32.

2. *Congressional Quarterly Almanac 1990* (Washington, D.C.: Congressional Quarterly, 1991), 76.

CHAPTER 4

Foreign Travel:

Business and Pleasure

"An overseas tour by a congressman or candidate," wrote William L. Safire, "is described by him as a fact-finding trip and as a junket by his opponents, who usually add 'at the taxpayer's expense.' "[1] Members who travel abroad at government expense defend the practice as a valuable way to learn about world problems, especially those that are debated in Congress. Detractors say such trips are usually a waste of taxpayers' money.

The critics haven't kept members at home. A Congressional Quarterly survey published in September 1989 found that House and Senate committees and special delegations reported spending $7.3 million in public funds on foreign travel in 1988.[2]

Members generally undertake foreign travel on committee business or by executive request or appointment. Travel reports detailing the costs of such trips must be made public annually. Travel reports do not have to be filed for foreign travel funded by the executive branch or by private organizations. However, members must include in their regular financial disclosure reports any privately funded foreign travel whose total value exceeded $250. *(Box, p. 39)*

PROS AND CONS OF FOREIGN TRAVEL

Ever since members of Congress began taking trips abroad at government expense, there have been opposing arguments on the value of such travel. Supporters defend foreign travel on three bases: fact-finding, overseeing government operations, and monitoring the administration of U.S. aid. Travel, these defenders argue, enables members to develop insights they would not otherwise obtain, and such firsthand information is needed for intelligent legislating. "It is absolutely preposterous for people to think [senators] can be well-informed without having visited the places they're making policy for. Senators are so insulated. . . . It makes sense to travel. It's stupid not to," said Sen. Joseph R. Biden, Jr., D-Del, in 1981.[3]

Legislators also note that the travel is not always the luxurious vacation that critics depict. Often tedious, occasionally arduous, foreign travel is sometimes dangerous. In 1989 Rep. Mickey Leland, D-Texas, was killed when his plane crashed in Ethiopia where he had been on a hunger relief mission. In 1978 Rep. Leo J. Ryan, D-Calif., was

Marty La Vor

Not all foreign trips are the luxurious junkets critics depict. Rep. Mickey Leland, D-Texas, was killed in a 1989 plane crash while on a hunger relief mission in Ethiopia.

shot and killed while investigating a religious cult in Guyana, South America.

Still, some foreign travel does have the appearance of being more pleasure than business, and some legislators try to win favor with their constituents on that fact. "I have taken no junkets, and will not, because I believe they are an outrageous waste of the taxpayers' money," said Rep. Ron Paul, R-Texas, in 1981. "At a time when average Americans can hardly afford to take a weekend from home, it is terrible for politicians to be taking lush vacations at the people's expense." [4]

Often cited as junkets are the annual trips members make to meetings of the Interparliamentary Union and the North Atlantic Assembly—organizations intended to bring U.S. and foreign legislators together—and the Paris International Air Show, where manufacturers display military hardware and other equipment.

Critics contend that legislators traveling abroad spend only a minimal amount of time on official business, make unreasonable demands on U.S. embassy personnel in the countries they visit, sometimes damage American prestige through tactless acts or comments while abroad, and often confound foreign officials by giving the

Types of Travel

The House Committee on Standards of Official Conduct lists eight types of travel that House members frequently engage in, both domestic and foreign. These are:

1. Official congressional travel, member's office. Travel to the district is authorized for a member and his staff in pursuit of the member's "official and representational duties." The member is not required to include this travel in his financial disclosure report; it is reported by the clerk of the House.

2. Official congressional travel, domestic committee business. This travel is permitted to members and committee staff members for official committee business, including hearings, studies, and the conduct of investigations. Such trips are reported by the clerk of the House.

3. Official congressional travel, foreign committee business. This travel is permitted to members for official business requested by the committee chairman. The traveler must submit an itemized report to the committee chairman.

4. Travel provided by a federal, state, or local government. Members are permitted to travel on official business at the request of a government. Travelers need not report travel sponsored by the federal government, but beginning in 1991 members must include travel sponsored by state or local governments in their financial disclosure statements.

5. Travel provided by a foreign government. As a general rule, a member may accept travel provided by a foreign government or a multinational organization only if the travel is wholly outside the United States. An exception is made for approved exchange programs. The member must report the travel within ten days to the Committee on Standards of Official Conduct.

6. Campaign and political travel. Travel is permitted for a bona fide campaign or political purpose and must be reported on Federal Election Commission reports.

7. Privately sponsored fact-finding travel. A House member and a spouse or another family member may accept travel paid for by a private organization for purposes "directly related" to official duties. Unless prior approval is obtained from the House Ethics Committee, the sponsor may pick up the tab for a maximum of four days, including travel time, if the trip is within the United States, and seven days, excluding travel time, if it is abroad.

8. Substantial participation in a private event. A member, accompanied by a spouse or other family member, may accept travel expenses from a private sponsor for speaking or otherwise substantially participating in a private event. As for privately sponsored fact-finding travel, a sponsor may pay for only four days' expenses if the trip is domestic, seven days if the trip is abroad.

House members are required to report in their financial disclosure statements any reimbursements for travel expenses from a single source that total $250 or more in any given year. Members may no longer accept honoraria for speeches or appearances, but they are allowed to request that charitable contributions be made in their name in lieu of honoraria.

Senate rules on travel are similar except for the limitations on what private organizations can pay for. Under Senate rules private sources can pay travel expenses for no more than three days of domestic travel and seven days for foreign trips. Both limits exclude travel time.

impression that their comments reflect official U.S. policy.

The use of "control rooms" is frequently cited as an example of extravagance and waste. Control rooms, often set up by military escort officers in the hotel where members are staying, provide an assembly point and a place to have coffee in the morning or cocktails at the end of the day.

Critics assert that this practice amounts to pampering Congress. Defenders counter that making legislators comfortable allows them to get more work done. They say that most members work hard and that the benefits of the trips far exceed the costs.

Most official trips are made under the auspices of congressional committees, although House and Senate leaders also get special travel allowances— and have often been criticized for how they have used them. In April 1981, for instance, Speaker Thomas P. O'Neill, Jr., D-Mass., and fourteen colleagues flew to New Zealand and Australia for two weeks to hold discussions with leaders in those countries on national security and economic issues. Many viewed the trip, which came in the midst of a congressional battle over President Ronald Reagan's program to cut the federal budget, as a blatant example of wasteful spending. Even some Democrats said O'Neill should have been in Washington lining up votes against the Reagan economic program.

Similar criticisms were voiced in 1988 when Speaker Jim Wright, D-Texas, invited thirteen members and seven staffers to accompany him to Australia for the centennial celebration of that country's parliament. In 1985 Rep. Bill Alexander, an Arkansas Democrat, used a military plane, at a cost of $50,000, for a solo trip to Brazil; Democratic colleagues later reacted by ousting him as chief deputy whip.

One of the most celebrated junketeers in congressional history was Rep. Adam Clayton Powell, Jr., D-N.Y. In one trip in 1962, Powell traveled through Europe for six weeks accompanied by two female assistants. According to one report, Powell requested State Department assistance in obtaining reservations at various European nightclubs and in arranging a six-day cruise on the Aegean Sea. Powell's extravagant travel contributed to his eventual ouster as chairman of the House Education and Labor Committee.

EFFORTS TO CONTROL TRAVEL

Congress first initiated some control over federally funded foreign travel when it passed the Mutual Security Act of 1954. In addition to appropriated funds, the act for the first time allowed congressional committees to use counterpart funds (foreign currencies credited to the United States in return for aid, which may be spent only in the country of origin). It also required legislators to make a full report to the House Administration Committee or the Senate Rules and Administration Committee on the amount of counterpart funds they spent. Beginning in 1959 these reports were required to be published annually in the *Congressional Record.*

It was not until 1961, however, that members were required to account publicly for appropriated funds they had spent on overseas trips. Not only committee reports but individual itemized expenditures of both appropriated and counterpart funds now had to be reported in the *Record.*

In 1963 the House took further steps to curb foreign travel by allowing only five House committees to use appropriated and counterpart funds for travel abroad. Ten other committees could sponsor foreign trips only with permission from the House Rules Committee. And in 1967 and 1968 the House took steps to curb abuses of per diem expenses.

In October 1973 Congress reversed field and, as part of the State Department authorization bill, eliminated the requirement that foreign travel reports from committees and individual members be published in the *Congressional Record.* Nor were the House and Senate oversight committees any longer required to make public a separate accounting of tax dollars spent on congressional travel.

The change was engineered by Rep. Wayne L. Hays, D-Ohio, chairman of the subcommittee in which the bill originated. Hays, who was also chairman of the House Administration Committee and a champion of generous perquisites for his colleagues, claimed his purpose was to trim the size of the *Record.* "We decided we weren't going to spend eight or nine thousand dollars to let you guys [reporters] do your stories on congressional travel," he said, adding that "there was no desire on anyone's part to cover up anything." [5]

Newspapers throughout the country editorialized against the change. As a result, in August 1974 Congress decided to make the reports public. But instead of requiring that they be published in the *Record,* which was readily available throughout the country, the reports were to be made available by the clerk of the House and the secretary of the Senate. In 1975 Hays gained control over the House reports when Congress specified that the reports be filed with the House Administration Committee, rather than the clerk's office.

Barely a year later, however, Hays was caught at the center of a sex-payroll scandal and was forced to resign as chairman of the House Administration Committee. In the aftermath of the scandal, Congress passed several reforms, including one that required the annual foreign travel expense reports prepared by House and Senate committees to be printed once again in the *Record.*

Basic disclosure laws for official foreign travel have remained the same since 1976. Annual reports published in the *Congressional Record* on travel by House committee members and other House delegations, such as those authorized by the Speaker, include the name of the members and committees aides, the time spent in each country, and the amount spent on per diem, transportation, and other expenses; the purpose of the trips is rarely reported, however. The reports must be submitted to the clerk of the House or the secretary of the Senate within sixty days of the beginning of each regular session of Congress.

NOTES

1. William L. Safire, *The New Language of Politics: A Dictionary of Catchwords, Slogans, and Political Usage,* rev. ed. (New York: Collier Books, 1972), 196.

2. Ronald D. Elving, "Junketing or Fact-Finding? Trips Pose Image Problem," *Congressional Quarterly Weekly Report,* September 2, 1989, 2240-2244.

3. Richard Whittle, "Maligned and Controversial, Congressional Travel May Decline in Popularity," *Congressional Quarterly Weekly Report,* August 22, 1981, 1543.

4. Whittle, "Maligned and Controversial, Congressional Travel May Decline in Popularity," 1542.

5. Congressional Quarterly, *Congress and the Nation,* vol. 4 (Washington, D.C.: Congressional Quarterly, 1977), 780.

CHAPTER 5

Official Allowances:

A Plethora of Privileges

The travel allowance provided in an act of September 22, 1789, fixing the compensation of members of Congress was the first of what has become a plethora of special allowances lawmakers have created for themselves through the years.

One of the biggest today is the official expense allowance, which is separate from the clerk-hire allowance senators and representatives receive for staff assistance. The expense allowance covers domestic travel, stationery, newsletters, postage, telephone and telegraph service, and office expenses in Washington, D.C., and in the member's congressional district or state.

In the 1970s both the House and Senate consolidated their allowances for basic office supplies and services, such as stationery, postage, computer services, telephone and telegraph, travel, office expenses in their state, and other official expenses, with no restrictions on the amount they could spend in any one category.

Until 1977 the House had nine separate special allowances, and representatives often had to adhere to certain limits on spending in each account. Special allowances generally were less generous and flexible for representatives than for senators. For example, most House allowances had to be spent a month at a time, whereas Senate allowances usually were cumulative over an entire calendar year. But the rules were changed in 1977, after Hays was forced to resign as chairman of the House Administration Committee, the panel that sets expense guidelines.

HOUSE EXPENSE ALLOWANCE

Separate House functions were consolidated into two main accounts: official expenses and clerk-hire allowances. Official expenses covered the costs incurred in running congressional offices, both in Washington and in members' home districts. The clerk-hire account was used to pay the eighteen permanent and four nonpermanent employees representatives are allowed to hire.

The consolidated account system replaced the nine separate special allowances for travel, office equipment leasing, district office leasing, telecommunications, stationery, constituent communications, postage, computer services, and other official expenses.

The size of House members' official expense allowance was determined by combining expenses in six fixed categories. Overall, the House allocated over $85 million in fiscal 1991 for official expenses. Each member was given a base of $67,000, plus additional expenditures for three variable allowances—travel, telephone and telegraph, and district office rental, the amount of which depended upon the location of a member's district and its distance from Washington, D.C. A California legislator, for example, received more than a New York legislator because the travel and telephone costs were higher.

Starting in 1977, members were required to file quarterly reports detailing how they were using their expense allowance. Official expenses were defined as "ordinary and necessary business expenses incurred by the member . . . in support of the member's official and representational duties."

The committee has also issued strict rules on what members can and cannot be reimbursed for. Under the panel's guidelines, House members could not be reimbursed from their expense accounts for the following types of expenditures:

- Employment service fees, moving allowances, and other expenses relating to hiring staff.
- Purchase or rental of items "having an extended useful life," such as the rental of a tuxedo. But members could charge office equipment relating to their duties to their official expense account.
- Greeting cards, flowers, trophies, donations, and dues for groups, other than congressional organizations approved by the House Administration Committee. (Members who had claimed these expenses protested that constituents expected their representatives to send flowers to funerals, award sports trophies, and join lodges.)
- Radio or television time or advertisements, except for notices of meetings relating to congressional business.
- Tuition or fees for education and training unless a need for a special skill, relating to House activities, could be proved.

Although expense guidelines are not listed within the official House rules, since being implemented in 1977 they have had the force of House rules. The House Administration Committee chairman would not sign vouchers for expenditures barred by the guidelines. If members labeled the proscribed expenditures as "political" and reported them as required by federal campaign statutes, they would have to pay the expenditures with campaign contributions.

Flexibility of Allowance

Although funds still are earmarked for some types of official expenses, the House Administration Committee has eliminated the requirement that separate records be kept for each category. Thus, all the money in the expense allowance can be used as each member sees fit, so long as it is spent for official expenses within the guidelines set by the committee.

With the consolidated system, it also is easier for members to use up their entire expense account funds each year since representatives may freely transfer funds from one category to another. And if the official expense account fund turns out to be insufficient, up to $50,000 of a member's clerk-hire funds may be transferred to the expense allowance. Conversely, members may use up to $50,000 of their expense allowance to pay for staff assistance.

House rules require members to submit documentation of expenses incurred in order to be reimbursed. The documentation is reviewed by the clerk's office but is not available for public inspection.

SENATE EXPENSE ALLOWANCE

The amount of a senator's expense allowance, like that for a representative, varies. For a senator it is determined by the size of his or her state and the distance between Washington, D.C., and the state. In 1989 the allowance ranged from $36,000 annually for a senator from Delaware to $156,000 annually for a senator from Hawaii. The dollar value of the allowance, payable from the contingent fund of the Senate, was determined by averaging the existing allowances for the two senators of each state, increasing that amount by 10 percent, and rounding the number up to the nearest $1,000. This was designed to increase senators' expense allowances while providing the same amount for both senators from a state.

According to the "Senate Handbook," prepared by the Senate Rules and Administration Committee, the Senatorial Official Office Expense Account is a "multipurpose account" authorized each year. At the end of the year, any unused balance may not be carried over to the next year.

Before 1979 a senator was able to request reimbursement for office expenses on his signature alone. The senator merely had to sign his name beneath a statement printed on an itemized voucher that said, "I certify that the above expenses were officially incurred." But the Senate has tightened its regulations on allowances by requiring senators to document each expense greater than $25. Expenses of $25 or less must either be itemized or documented. The rules also require each voucher requesting reimbursement to be "personally signed" by a senator.

The Senate expense allowance may be used for official telegrams and long-distance phone calls and related services; phone calls incurred outside of Washington; stationery and office supplies purchased through the Senate Stationery Room for official business; any type of postal service or private mail delivery service relating to official business; district office expenses other than equipment and furniture; subscriptions to newspapers, clipping services, and periodicals; official travel; expenses incurred by individuals selected by a senator to serve on panels or other bodies making

recommendations on nominees to the service academies or federal judgeships; and "other official expenses as the senator determines are necessary."

There is no limit on the amount that can be spent in any one category, except for the latter category of "other official expenses." That discretionary allowance is unique to the Senate and permits a senator to spend up to 10 percent of his or her total available funds for any "official expenses."

Definition of Official Expenses

Though the Senate spends millions of dollars annually on "official expenses," until the last decade it had never defined what was an official expense. Finally, in 1980, the Senate agreed that official expenses were "ordinary and necessary business expenses incurred by a senator and his staff in the discharge of their official duties."

The following expenses specifically were excluded: commuting and commuter parking fees; greeting cards; flowers; trophies; awards or certificates; donations or gifts of any type (except gifts of flags flown over the United States Capitol, and copies of an illustrated history book of Congress entitled *We, the People*); dues or assessments; broadcast or print advertising time except for help-wanted ads; expenses incurred by an individual who is not an employee (except those individuals selected by a senator to serve on panels or other bodies making recommendations on nominees to service academies or federal judgeships); salaries or compensation of employees; entertainment; meals; private automobile maintenance; and employee moving expenses, including travel.

A subsequent revision adopted by the Senate excluded supplemental allowances—which are separate from the expense allowances—given the vice president, president pro tempore, majority and minority leaders, and majority and minority whips.

Members' Allowances

Legislators have given themselves a variety of expense allowances. Today they are generally considered a necessary accessory to members' regular salary. They range from generous staff assistance and office space to free use of video recording facilities and sophisticated computer services. Congressional leaders receive additional remuneration.

Listed below are the major allowances and, where available, the dollar value of those benefits as of 1990. No value is given to some of the allowances because of the difficulty in determining the range of reimbursed costs, such as for travel and telephone usage. Most of the allowances were transferable from one account to another.

	House	Senate
Washington office clerk-hire	$379,480	$716,102-1,458,856[1]
Committee legislative assistants	—[3]	$243,543
General office expenses	$67,000	$36,000-156,000[1]
Telephone/telegraph	15,000 long-distance minutes to district	—[2]
Stationery	—[2]	—[4]
Office space	2-3 room suites	5-8 room suites
Furnishings	provided	provided
Equipment	—[2]	provided
District/state offices		
Rental	2,500 sq. ft.	4,800-8,000 sq. ft.[1]
Furnishings/equipment	$35,000	$30,000-41,744[1]
Mobile office	—[2]	one
Communications		
Automated correspondence	—[2]	provided by Senate computer center
Audio/video recordings; photography	—[2]	—[2]
Travel	formula (min. $6,200-max. $67,200[5])	—[2]

1. Senators are allowed expenses based on a sliding scale linked to the state's population.

2. Expenses are covered through the general office expenses line item. In most cases supplies and equipment are charged at rates well below retail levels.

3. Provided for members of Appropriations, Budget, and Rules committees.

4. Senators pay for stationery out of their official expenses allowance and receive in addition allotments of white envelopes and letterheads, blank sheets, and brown "public documents" envelopes based on the state's population.

5. Excluding Alaska, Hawaii, and U.S. territories.

Source: Adapted from Roger H. Davidson and Walter J. Oleszek, *Congress and Its Members,* 3d ed. (Washington, D.C.: CQ Press, 1990), 141.

DOMESTIC TRAVEL ALLOWANCE

The restrictions on congressional travel have eased a great deal. In the early 1960s senators and representatives were allowed three government-paid trips home each year. The number was raised repeatedly in the following two decades so that by the late 1970s senators could take more than forty trips home and representatives were allowed thirty-three. By 1980 there were no limits on the number of trips that could be taken.

House

Travel allowances are calculated based on the proximity of the member's district to Washington,

D.C. Before expense accounts were consolidated in 1977, representatives received a separate travel allowance that permitted them twenty-six free round trips each year to and from their home district plus extra trips for their staffs.

Members could also choose to withdraw their travel allowance in cash, up to a maximum of $2,250 a year; any amount not used for travel could go toward members' personal expenses so long as they paid income taxes on it. Changes to the rules in 1976 ended the "cash-out" option.

The House calculates a domestic travel allowance for each member and uses that figure in determining the official expense allowances. In 1991 that figure was the equivalent of sixty-four multiplied by the rate per mile (23 cents per mile for 3,000 miles or over, and 39 cents per mile for travel under 500 miles), multiplied by the mileage between the District of Columbia and the farthest point in the member's district, plus 10 percent. This works out to roughly thirty-two round trips a year. If a member's travel exceeds thirty-two round trips a year, other funds from the official expense allowance may be used.

Members are reimbursed for the actual cost of travel, including rail and air fare, food, and lodging. When a member travels in a privately owned or leased automobile, he is reimbursed at a rate of 25.5 cents per mile for 15,000 miles or less; 11 cents for over 15,000 miles. Members also may be reimbursed for travel on official business that is in addition to visits to their home district or states. For official committee business, a member receives $70 per diem for domestic travel.

The Defense Department also provides members of Congress with free transportation in the line of official business. But department officials do not release figures on the cost of such special shuttle service.

A discount airfare program offered by some commercial air carriers is available to House members and staff traveling on official business.

Senate

Travel is one of several items authorized as part of senators' official expense accounts. Reimbursable travel expenses include:

- Per diem and actual transportation expenses. The maximum per diem within the continental United States in 1991 was $110 (the rate differed in Alaska and Hawaii). Per diem expenses covered food, lodging, tips, laundry, and other incidental charges. There was no reimbursement for entertainment, nor could reimbursement for transportation (air and rail fare) exceed actual expenses. Under previous rules reimbursement claims had been limited under certain circumstances to less than actual expenses.
- Privately owned automobile mileage not to exceed 25 cents per mile.
- Motorcycle mileage not to exceed 25 cents per mile.
- Airplane mileage not to exceed 60 cents per mile.
- Actual costs of parking fees, ferry fares, and bridge, road, and tunnel tolls.

There is a statutory travel allowance for one round trip between a senator's home and Washington, D.C., which is paid to senators at the beginning of each regular session of Congress. Reimbursement for this travel is 25 cents per mile; mileage is calculated by the nearest route usually traveled by a senator in going to his home state and returning to Washington. This reimbursement is automatic; it is not paid from the official office expense account, and no voucher is submitted.

The travel allowance for each senator used to be based on the cost of forty round trips a year for states with fewer than 10 million people and forty-four round trips for states with more than 10 million. A state's distance from Washington was figured in the computation. The travel allowance for senators no longer sets limits on the number of trips that can be taken each year. Senate regulations state that office staff must make round trips since the Senate will not pay the expenses of aides who relocate—for example, a staffer who moves to Washington after serving in a member's district office. (Although the House does not have any specific regulation governing round trips for staff, it also does not pay personnel relocation costs.)

Unlike the House, the Senate will reimburse for travel expenses that include official travel anywhere within the United States. (Before 1977 senators could only be reimbursed for travel within or to a senator's home state.) It also authorized per diem expenses for travel within a senator's home state. But neither the travel allowance nor the per diem allowance were permitted in the sixty-day period immediately prior to a contested primary or general election in which the senator was a candidate for office. In addition, the Senate required members to make public how they used the per diem and travel allowance funds.

A discount airfare program offered by some commercial air carriers is available to senators and employees traveling on "official business only." Senators also can accept free domestic transportation from the Defense Department or company noncommercial carriers.

STATIONERY, NEWSLETTERS, AND POSTAGE

House

A representative's funds for stationery, postage, and newsletters come from his official expense account. There is no limit, within the account, on the amount he can spend on any one item. *(Official expense account allowance, box, p. 46)*

By 1991 the base amount of a representative's official expense account came to $67,000. (The size of the allowance varies from representative to representative, depending on distance between Washington and the member's congressional district.)

In addition to his expense account, each representative is allowed forty thousand "Public Document" envelopes a month without charge.

In 1989 and 1990 curbs were placed on mailing privileges for both House and Senate members. For the first time separate House and Senate "franking" accounts were established, with the belief that it would make each member more accountable for the spending. *(Franking privilege, p. 27)*

The franking privilege has always been a frequent target of criticism for its abuse in reelection efforts—particularly from Republicans frustrated by their party's difficulty in ousting Democratic incumbents.

For the most part, attempts to keep down mail spending worked. In fiscal 1991 the House appropriated $59 million for franking costs—the lowest level in years. In fiscal 1992 franking was set at $80 million, which was the lowest level for an election year since 1982.

For years many lame duck members also have been criticized for taking their remaining expense account funds in the form of postage stamps. Critics have argued that lame duck representatives do not need regular postage because they are allowed to use the frank for ninety days after they leave office to clean up all remaining official correspondence.

Senate

Funds for Senate stationery and postage come from the member's consolidated office expense account. Each senator also receives allotments of white envelopes and letterheads, blank sheets, and brown "Public Document" envelopes, all based on the state's population.

Some services for printing and bulk mailing of

R. Michael Jenkins

Moving day, 1991: staff of Rep. Jim Slattery, D-Kan., sets up shop in a new office.

newsletters, questionnaires, excerpts from the *Congressional Record,* and other items are provided without charge by the Senate's Service Department.

As in the House, changes to franking rules have held down spending. Mail spending was just $17 million in fiscal 1990 after senators were forced to disclose individual spending.

TELEPHONE AND TELEGRAPH ALLOWANCE

House

In computing the yearly telephone allowance for representatives in 1991, the following formula was used: the dollar equivalent of 15,000 multiplied by the daytime person-to-person rate per minute from the District of Columbia to the member's district. A member may elect to use more than this amount on calls so long as total expenses in all official expense account categories do not exceed his or her established allowance.

Starting in 1976, each member was permitted to have two wide-area telephone service (WATS) lines to reduce costs for long-distance calls. If a representative chose to use WATS lines, half the annual telecommunications allowance had to be given up, although with a $6,000 floor.

Senate

Since the Senate consolidated accounts in 1973, the Rules and Administration Committee has fixed senators' telephone and telegraph rates. The allowance was based on a fixed number of long-distance calls totaling no more than a fixed number of minutes for calls to and from Washington. The committee used a complicated formula to determine the telegraph allowance, based on state population and Western Union rates from Washington. Both formulas were used to determine a senator's total consolidated allowance, now called the official office expense account.

Many senators have access either to a nationwide Federal Telecommunications System (FTS) leased line or a WATS line provided by the telephone companies. Each senator (including those from Alaska and Hawaii) is permitted two WATS lines in his or her Washington office, the cost of which is not charged against the senator's official office expense account.

OFFICE ALLOWANCES

House

The Washington office of a representative, typically a two- or three-room suite, is provided free of charge. Office furnishings and decorations, housekeeping, and maintenance also are provided at no cost to the member. Additional storage space and trunks are available free of charge. Representatives pay for electrical and mechanical office equipment, including computers, from their official expense account.

In recent years a handful of representatives have used their office expense accounts to pay for outside consultants, who are hired to help them cope with the organizational demands of running a congressional office. Consultants have set up the Washington offices of freshmen representatives, trained new staffers, and improved mail flow, among other things. Neither the consulting firms nor the members utilizing this service are eager to advertise this use of the expense account since consultants are expensive.

For their districts, members are given an allowance designed to cover up to 2,500 square feet of office space. Unused funds could be transferred within a member's consolidated office account and used for other office expenses.

The Washington offices and furnishings for senators are provided free, as are housekeeping and maintenance services. Senators do not have allowances to buy or lease office equipment; it is provided by the sergeant at arms of the Senate.

A senator's home state office space is allocated according to the state's population. Within the allowed square footage there is no limit to the number of offices he may open. Offices are provided free in federal buildings or leased from private owners at the General Services Administration (GSA) regional rate. Senators receive an aggregate furniture and equipment allowance. The minimum allowance is $30,000 for 4,800 square feet, which is the amount received by senators from the smallest states. The amount is increased for each authorized increase of square feet. All furnishings are provided through GSA. Each senator also is allowed to rent one mobile office for use throughout the state.

Rent and furnishings for senators' state offices are not chargeable to the official office account. These allowances also are provided through the GSA and are paid for by the Senate sergeant at arms.

PUBLICATIONS ALLOWANCE

In addition to their official expense allowance covering office operations, communications, and travel, members of Congress receive a number of free publications. Some are used directly in the member's work—for example, a complete set of the U.S. Code and District of Columbia codes and supplements, four subscriptions to the *Federal Register,* and office copies of the *Congressional Record* and the *Congressional Directory*. All of these publications are printed by the United States Government Printing Office.

Representatives are allotted thirty-four subscriptions to the *Record;* senators are allotted fifty.

Each senator and representative receives a clothbound copy of the annual *Congressional Directory,* with his or her name engraved on it. Each senator's office receives fifteen paperbound copies; an additional forty copies may be distributed by each senator. Representatives receive ten paperbound copies for their offices; they are permitted to distribute an additional twenty copies.

Members also receive allotments of special publications to send off to constituents. One of the most popular is the *Yearbook* of the Department of Agriculture. Each representative is allotted four hundred copies, worth $4,800. Senators have an allotment of 550. Unused *Yearbooks* and certain other publications may be turned in to the Government Printing Office for exchange or credit toward other books or pamphlets.

Among other items members may choose to distribute are pamphlets on American history, the legislative process, historic documents, and calendars, including "We, the People" wall calendars.

"We, the People" calendars are full-color, glossy photo calendars that carry the name of the member. They are published by the U.S. Capitol Historical Society and are a big hit with constituents. "No other comparable document receives such acclaim," said Rep. Joseph M. Gaydos, D-Pa., chairman of a House Administration subcommittee. "We print a very limited number. I wish we could double or triple it," Gaydos said.

Members of Congress are entitled to goatskin-bound copies of any one of some 25,000 different documents stocked by the Government Printing Office. Senators and representatives also receive an unabridged dictionary and stand as part of their office furnishings.

Chapter 6

Additional Benefits:

Congressional Privilege

In addition to their expense allowances, foreign travel compensation, and franking privileges, members of Congress benefit from numerous services, courtesies, and special favors that go along with the job. Because of the difficulty of defining and isolating types of benefits, it is not possible to compile a complete list or compute their precise value. Selected additional benefits are described below.

CONGRESSIONAL BENEFITS

Life Insurance

Regardless of age or state of health, every member receives term life insurance under the Federal Employees Group Life Insurance. The amount of the policy, which is pegged to annual salary, is $128,000 for each member. The government pays one-third of the premium of the basic plan.

Additional $10,000 policies as well as coverage of from two to five times a member's annual pay are available, with the extra premiums determined by the age of the member. Family members also are eligible under these plans. Members pay the full cost of the premiums for the additional policies.

Health Insurance

Under the Federal Employees Health Benefits Program, lawmakers are eligible for a variety of health insurance plans. The government contributions toward these plans vary, but they cannot exceed 75 percent of a member's insurance premium.

Capitol Hill Health Facilities

A staff of doctors, nurses, and other medical personnel stands by in the Capitol to give members free medical care while at work. The Office of the Attending Physician is staffed and operated by the navy.

Services that are available to senators and representatives include physical examinations, laboratory work, x-ray services, electrocardiograms, periodic health preventive programs, physiotherapy, immunizations for foreign travel, ambulance service, allergy injections, and supplies of prescription medicines. First aid stations found in every House and Senate office building offer help to members, their staffs, and visitors for minor ailments.

The Cost of Congress

The cost of running Congress has grown dramatically in the last three decades. In fiscal 1960 the legislative budget—including the operations of Congress and the related agencies—totaled $128.8 million; by fiscal 1991 that figure had jumped to approximately $2.2 billion. The increase reflected the growth of the legislative bureaucracy. In 1960 House and Senate employees numbered about 6,300; some thirty years later that total exceeded 17,300.

The legislative branch, like any other government agency, must request funds for its own programs and activities in an annual budget. The process generally is the same as that for the executive branch departments: Proposed funding for Congress and related agencies is incorporated in a legislative appropriations bill, which must be approved by the House and Senate. Neither chamber, as a general rule, delves into the requests and operations of the other, and the executive branch does not review congressional funding decisions.

Fiscal 1960 Legislative Funds

Senate	$26,406,345
House of Representatives	42,398,065
Capitol Police	143,135
Joint Committee on Reduction of Nonessential Federal Expenditures	24,795
Education of Pages	62,500
Miscellaneous	2,699,000
Architect of the Capitol	27,412,900
Botanic Garden	327,500
Library of Congress	14,302,790
Government Printing Office	15,020,350
Total	**$128,797,380***

* Does not include $41,800,000 in funding for the General Accounting Office.

Fiscal 1991 Legislative Funds

Congressional Operations	
Senate	$437,223,000
House of Representatives	647,675,000
Joint Items	114,187,000
Office of Technology Assessment	19,557,000
Congressional Budget Office	21,183,000
Architect of the Capitol	139,806,000
Congressional Research Service	52,743,000
Government Printing Office (congressional printing)	79,615,000
Related Agencies	
Botanic Garden	3,519,000
Library of Congress	239,924,000
Architect of the Capitol (library buildings)	15,268,000
Copyright Royalty Tribunal	127,000
Government Printing Office (noncongressional printing)	26,500,000
General Accounting Office	419,130,000
Total	**$2,216,457,000**

Library Services

The Library of Congress provides senators and representatives with valuable information resources. This includes free research services and facilities, free speechwriting, and free materials that can be sent to constituents or used to answer constituents' questions. There are more than eight hundred employees at the Library's Congressional Research Service who work exclusively for members of Congress.

Surplus Books

The Library of Congress gives away to members and their staffs surplus books that are not suitable for the library's collections. Most of these volumes are duplicate copies of books already held by the library or discarded publications sent from various agencies or offices. Members may select and keep books for their own use or send volumes to libraries and schools in their districts or states. *(See also free publications, p. 50)*

Legislative Counsel

The Office of Legislative Counsel, which has offices located on both sides of Capitol Hill, assists members of Congress in drafting bills, resolutions, and amendments. Its staff provides confidential help to committees and members on legislative matters only; it does not perform personal legal work for members.

Legal Counsel

The Office of Senate Legal Counsel, created by the Ethics in Government Act of 1978, provides advice and handles legal matters relating to official work of Senate members, committees, and staffers. Functions of the office include defending the Senate against outside suits; the filing of civil actions to enforce subpoenas; and the identification of pending legal proceedings that might affect congressional powers and responsibilities. The House counterpart to the Senate's legal counsel is the general counsel in the office of the clerk.

Chaplains

Both the House and Senate have their own chaplain, who is responsible for opening each daily session with a prayer and for serving generally as spiritual counselor to members, their families, and their staffs. The chaplains are officers of their respective chambers. In 1991 the House chaplain received a salary of $115,092; the Senate chaplain, $88,687.

Tax Preparation

The Internal Revenue Service maintains a temporary office in both the House and Senate between January and April each year to help members and staff prepare their income tax returns. The public criticism of the special services these offices provide for members and staff has resulted in demands that the IRS close these facilities.

Recreation

Members of Congress have their own free health club, including a modern gymnasium in the Rayburn House Office Building and an exercise room in the Russell Senate Office Building. Facilities include swimming pools, exercise machines, and saunas as well as court facilities for volleyball, paddleball, and basketball.

Capitol Hill Restaurants

Government-subsidized food and eating facilities are available to members, staff, and visitors. The Capitol and congressional office buildings contain five public restaurants and cafeterias; five restaurants for members, senior staff, and their guests; and eight carry-out services. In addition, members may reserve several private dining rooms or arrange banquets and parties in caucus rooms with low-cost catering from the House and Senate restaurants.

The House restaurants operate from a "revolving fund," and all operating expenditures are paid from restaurant revenues. Senate restaurants also operate from a revolving fund, but some funds are appropriated each year for management employees and equipment maintenance. Congress provides the restaurants with the space, utilities, janitorial, and other services, and the Government Printing Office prints the menus—all at no charge to the restaurants.

Merchandise Discounts

Stationery stores located in the House and Senate office buildings sell many gift items as well as normal office supplies, all at cost or slightly above. Members, their spouses, and their staffs can buy such things as wallets, briefcases, pocket calculators, and drinking glasses and ashtrays with the seal of either the House or the Senate. Christmas cards also are available at bargain prices.

Free Parking

Each representative gets a free Capitol Hill garage space for personal use, plus four additional spaces and one outside parking permit for staff use. Senators receive two parking spaces each, plus a limited number of outside permits for staff. By 1991 parking rates around Capitol Hill ranged from $65 to $125 a month, and parking spaces in prime business areas in Washington were rented for as high as $156 a month. Members may have their cars washed and waxed in the garages at discount prices. Free parking for an unlimited time period is provided for members at Washington-area airports (National, Dulles, and Baltimore-Washington International).

Capitol Waiting Areas

Congress provides attractive waiting rooms in the Capitol for members' spouses and families. The Senate Ladies Lounge and the Members' Family Suite (House) are located near each chamber's galleries.

Grooming

The House and Senate provide six barber and beauty shops in the Capitol and office buildings that give haircuts to members and staff. While charges for haircuts formerly were at reduced rates, all of these facilities in 1991 maintained their prices were comparable to those in the Washington area.

Office Decorations

The U.S. Botanic Garden will loan to members' offices six potted plants per year and provide floral centerpieces for official functions. Members may request cut flowers as well.

Members may decorate their offices with free wall maps and charts, scenic photographs, and reproductions of paintings and prints, all of which may be framed and installed at no cost to members. There are quotas on paintings and certain maps. Picture framing services also are available.

Ticket Offices

Two ticket offices run by the airlines in the Longworth (House) and Russell (Senate) office buildings and an Amtrak railroad ticket office in the Capitol make reservations and issue tickets for members. Special rates for rail travel are available for members traveling on official government business between Washington, D.C., and New York, N.Y. Congress provides these offices with operating space, utilities, and janitorial services.

Photographs

Both the House and Senate provide official photographic services at public expense for members. Members may have photographs taken with constituents and at official functions or ceremonial events for news and publicity use. The Senate and House have separate staff darkrooms. There are no longer separate studios for the Democrats and Republicans.

Senators purchase photographic services through their expense accounts or excess campaign funds. The money is put into a photographic/recording studio revolving fund and is used to purchase photographic supplies. House funds are used to purchase cameras, film, and supplies.

Recording Studios

Both the House and Senate have extensive radio and television recording facilities that are available to all members. In theory the recording studios are designed to help members communicate with their constituents. Radio or television tapes recorded at the studios can be mailed to local stations for use in local news or public affairs programming.

The studios produce radio programs and videotape programs for television, usually within twenty-four hours. The studios also are equipped with speaker-phone service for two-way interviews with local radio or TV stations. In all cases, members must design their own programs and write their own scripts, but the studios provide such services as teleprompters and set makeup. Members must make appointments for filming and taping; appointments may be made on a standing basis.

Studio productions are subsidized with public funds. Tapes and films are produced at cost, and representatives and senators may use their expense allowances to purchase audio and videotapes.

OTHER BENEFITS

Miscellaneous services and perquisites available to members include:

- Special congressional license tags provided by the city permit unrestricted parking by members on official business anywhere in Washington.
- American flags that have flown over the Capitol and certified by the Architect of the Capitol may be purchased at cost and presented as gifts.
- Members and staff may have packages wrapped free of charge for mailing, a service used heavily during the Christmas season.

CHAPTER 7

Patronage:

Waning Advantage of Office

Once one of the major advantages of holding public office, political patronage, especially that dispensed by members of Congress, has declined to virtually nothing. Unlike many of the other vanishing perks, the loss of patronage has not been particularly lamented; many legislators regarded it as a nuisance.

Senators and representatives were once able to pull the political strings on thousands of federal jobs. On Capitol Hill and back in their home states, a powerful member could place scores of people in such jobs as local postmaster, health inspector, tax collector, welfare commissioner, and even custodian of public morals. The congressional patronage empire thus provided members with a long list of jobs with which to pay off political supporters.

Today on Capitol Hill the only jobs remaining under patronage are those that do not require specialized skills or technical knowledge. These include elevator operators, doorkeepers, mail carriers, and clerks. All in all, a member now finds the available patronage jobs of little help in strengthening his political position or rewarding his campaign supporters back home.

GROWTH AND DECLINE

The practice of considering political loyalty when filling jobs began with President George Washington, but Andrew Jackson was the first president to openly back political patronage. Convinced that political loyalty was of paramount importance, he made a clean sweep of the government and filled vacancies with his men at all levels. But when Jackson spoke out in favor of patronage, the number of government jobs requiring technical skills was not large. The few misfits given menial jobs through patronage appointments seemed to do little damage to the general efficiency of the government.

As the business of government expanded and grew more complex, the inadequacies of a system that put a premium on loyalty rather than ability became glaringly apparent. Criticism of patronage increased sharply after the assassination of President James A. Garfield by a disappointed job seeker in 1881. In response, Congress enacted the first major civil service reform in America. The 1883 Pendleton Act set up a three-member bipartisan board, the Civil Service Commission, and gave it authority to certify applicants for federal employment after they took competitive examinations.

As Youngest Patronage Appointees, Capitol Pages Perform Many Errands

The youngest patronage employees on Capitol Hill are the House and Senate pages, who serve as messengers and perform other errands for members of Congress. Pages must be juniors in high school; they serve for at least one semester, and some stay for a full year. They attend school early in the morning and then go to work in the Capitol, where until early evening, or later if there is a night session, they answer phones, run errands, deliver messages, or distribute information. A House description of the page program, noting the extensive walking required on the job, said, "We cannot stress enough that pages bring well broken-in, comfortable shoes."

Although demands on a page's time are high, hundreds of young men and women vie for the positions each year. Those nominated by more senior legislators have the best chance of being selected to fill the approximately sixty-five page positions in the House and thirty in the Senate. The opportunity to observe Congress is unsurpassed, and the pay is good for people so young. In 1991 House pages earned $10,808 a year, and Senate pages earned $11,657. Pages are housed on two floors of a congressional office building.

History of Pages

Working as a page has not always been so lucrative. Congress has always used messengers, but the earliest record of boys filling these positions was in 1827, when three youngsters were employed as "runners" in the House.

Many of the runners were orphans or children of poor families, whose plight had come to the attention of a representative. There was apparently no law authorizing the use of young boys for these patronage jobs, yet hundreds were appointed over the years as a matter of practice. Members often paid the boys a bonus if they performed their duties well, but this practice was discontinued in 1843 after a special review of financial allocations in the House.

The Senate's first runner was nine-year-old Grafton Hanson, who was appointed under the august sponsorship of Senators Daniel Webster and Henry Clay. Hanson served his sponsors for ten years and later became Senate postmaster.

The name "pages" appeared first in the *Congressional Globe,* predecessor of the *Congressional Record,* of the 26th Congress (1839-1841). At about that time, a page was paid $1.50 a day.

A dress code was established for pages during the era when knickers were in vogue for boys. Until 1963, the Supreme Court, which had a small corps of pages until 1975, required its pages to wear knickers, long black stockings, and double-breasted jackets. Even more remarkable, until 1950, court pages could be no taller than five feet, four inches—the height of the backs of the justices' chairs.

Today, House and Senate pages wear dark blue suits, black ties, black shoes and socks, and long-sleeved white shirts. They do not have to wear their jackets at all times. The code is the same for both males and females.

Until 1971 all pages were boys. In December 1970 Sen. Jacob K. Javits, R-N.Y., appointed the first girl page, but she was not allowed to serve until May 1971, after the Senate passed a resolution permitting the appointment of female pages in the Senate. Earlier Javits broke another long-standing tradition, appointing in 1965 the first black page in congressional history.

Page Duties

Pages are under the direction of the House doorkeeper or the Senate sergeant at arms. Pages assigned to the House and Senate floors distribute pertinent documents to each legislator's seat in preparation for the day's business. When the House is called to order, the pages retire to a bench in the rear of the chamber to await a representative's call. A button next to a member's seat triggers a light on a board in the rear of the chamber signaling that a page is wanted. Senate pages sit on the rostrum at the front of the chamber and are called to run errands by the snapping of a senator's fingers. Other pages in both chambers may answer phones in the minority or majority cloakroom, deliver messages, and distribute documents.

Pages are also required to attend school. Not until the Legislative Reorganization Act of 1946 became law were pages provided with any kind of uniform schooling. They had to rely on private tutors if they wanted to

Senate pages pose on the Capitol steps with Vice President Thomas R. Marshall, who entertained them at Christmas dinner.

continue their education while working on Capitol Hill. With passage of the 1946 act, however, Congress set up the Capitol Page School in the Library of Congress, which was a public school operated by the District of Columbia with money appropriated for the purpose.

Scandals in the Early 1980s

Two related scandals in the early 1980s led to several changes in the page program. In news reports in 1982, two unidentified pages told of sexual misconduct on the part of House members involving pages. Later, after a House investigation, the two recanted their stories. Joseph A. Califano, Jr., a former cabinet secretary who headed the investigation, said most of "the allegations and rumors of misconduct were the product of teenage exaggeration, gossip, or even out-and-out fabrication that was often repeated mercilessly in a political capital that thrives on rumor."

In 1983, however, the House censured two of its members after the House Committee on Standards of Official Conduct reported that they had sexual relations with pages. Daniel B. Crane, an Illinois Republican with a wife and six children, admitted that he had had an affair in 1980 with a seventeen-year-old female page. Gerry E. Studds, a Massachusetts Democrat, was found to have had a homosexual relationship in 1973 with a seventeen-year-old male page.

As a result of these scandals, Congress agreed that only juniors in high school should serve as pages. Previously, pages had ranged in age from fourteen to eighteen, which, among other things, made it difficult to provide an appropriate school curriculum.

Congress also set up the Page Residence Hall in early 1983 and set curfews. Before then pages were required to find their own housing and provide their own meals.

Some members still argued that the page system should be abolished and the pages' duties taken over by adults.

The 1883 act covered only about 10 percent of federal employees in the executive branch, but its key provision gave the president power to expand the civil service classifications by executive order. A series of such orders, and additional legislation in the years that followed, removed from politics nearly all nonpolicy-making jobs in the federal government.

The last blow to the patronage system was dealt in 1969, when the Nixon administration decided to remove 63,000 postmaster and rural carrier appointments from politics. Instead, special boards were set up to select candidates for these positions. The Postal Reorganization Act of 1970, which established the U.S. Postal Service, put an end to patronage in the post office.

While the value of patronage to members declined, Congress retained an influential voice in presidential appointments to high-level government positions. Jobs filled by the administration in that category today include cabinet and subcabinet positions, the federal judiciary, major diplomatic and military posts, and top positions on independent boards and regulatory agencies, as well as some lesser positions exempt from the civil service.

Most of those appointments require Senate confirmation, although the administration is not required to consult with Congress before submitting its selections. The degree of influence a member has over those nominations generally depends on his personal relationship with the president and his power on Capitol Hill.

The tradition of "senatorial courtesy" still plays a role in some nominations.

In contrast to the executive branch, most congressional employees can be hired and fired at the whim of the members who employ them.

They do not enjoy the elaborate job security provided by civil service regulations covering job qualifications, equitable application procedures, minimum starting salaries, and the specific pay raise and promotion policies of the executive branch.

ALLOCATING PATRONAGE JOBS

The few hundred patronage positions that still exist are meted out to members of Congress under a bewildering combination of written rules and traditions that often contradict each other. The exceptions to the written procedures are so numerous and diverse that they have all but supplanted the rules.

Of the two chambers, the House has the more clearly defined method for distributing patronage jobs among its members. Since the Democrats gained control of the House in 1955, the Democratic Personnel Committee has controlled all patronage jobs. It assigns a small quota of the jobs to the minority party at the beginning of each session. These include such positions as clerk or page in the minority cloakroom. The remaining patronage jobs are allocated largely on the basis of seniority, although this is not a formal rule.

The patronage committee was first established by a caucus of Democratic representatives in 1911. When the Republicans gained control of the House in 1918, they set up their own patronage committee with rules that generally followed the Democrats' practices. The Republicans disbanded their committee in the early 1980s.

In the Senate, patronage allocation is handled through the office of the secretary of the majority party, which gives the sergeant at arms a list of those senators entitled to patronage slots. As in the House, seniority is the general criterion used for distributing patronage. The minority is entitled to fill one-third of the patronage positions; these are allocated through the office of the minority party secretary.

The office of the doorkeeper is responsible for overseeing the largest number of patronage jobs in the House. Most of the 381 positions authorized in 1991 were filled through patronage. The doorkeeper supervises the officers of the press galleries, the doormen for the visitors' gallery and for the House chamber, the custodians, barbers, pages, and employees of the House document room, and the folding room, which distributes newsletters, speeches, and other materials for representatives.

The sergeant at arms of the Senate supervises most of the patronage appointments in the Senate, including the Senate pages, doormen, elevator operators, custodians, officers of the Senate press galleries, and employees of the Senate post office.

Patronage in the Capitol Police force was sharply reduced in the early 1970s. In 1971 patronage appointments constituted 25 percent of the total force. By 1991 the number of patronage appointments had fallen to less than 10 percent of the total, and patronage appointees were required to meet the same standards and to undergo the same training as other members of the Capitol Police.

Although they are not technically patronage employees, there is a small group of Capitol Hill officials whose jobs depend on the influence of sponsors or on the party in control and the favor of the party leadership. The House doorkeeper, the House and Senate sergeants at arms, the secretary of the Senate, and the clerk of the House work for all members of their respective houses, but they are elected by the members on strict party-line votes.

APPOINTMENTS TO MILITARY ACADEMIES

One remnant of the patronage system continues to flourish. Congressional appointees to the three major service academies account for about three-fourths of these academies' combined enrollment. Although occasional efforts have been made to remove all academy appointments from the patronage system, members of Congress have been reluctant to let the last sizable group in the congressional patronage system slip away from them.

Until 1902 the privilege of appointing candidates for admission to the academies was enjoyed only by representatives, the idea being to apportion academy enrollment on the basis of national population. Each congressional district was to supply one appointee every four years, thus giving each class maximum geographic variance and assuring equal distribution of appointments throughout the nation.

Eventually senators and representatives alike were authorized to have as many as five appointees enrolled at each academy at one time. In 1990-91 the total enrollment at the U.S. Military Academy at West Point, New York, was set by law at 4,386. Of that number, about 60 percent were congressional appointees. The maximum number of cadets at the U.S. Naval Academy at Annapolis, Maryland, was set at 4,000 in 1990-91, 2,675 of whom could be appointed by Congress. About 80 percent of the 4,462 cadets enrolled at the U.S. Air Force Academy at Colorado Springs, Colorado, in 1990-91 were congressional appointees.

No candidate for appointment to the academies may be older than twenty-one. He or she must be "of good moral character, a U.S. citizen, and unmarried with no dependents. Candidates must also pass a medical examination and physical and scholastic aptitude tests. Within those minimum standards, members of Congress have great leeway in making their appointments. Most senators and many representatives do not personally handle the screening of applicants, but leave the job to an assistant in the state or district office.

Legislators may also nominate as many as ten candidates for appointment to the Merchant Marine Academy in Kings Point, New York. The candidates must take a nationally competitive examination to win appointment. No nominee on the member's list is guaranteed appointment; instead, the highest-scoring candidates are appointed to the freshman class, regardless of who nominated them. Members of Congress play no role in the selection of candidates to the U.S. Coast Guard Academy at New London, Connecticut.

CHAPTER 8

Congressional Staff:

A Member's Right Arm

One of the perquisites of office that members of Congress value most highly is congressional staff. Members rely heavily on staff during all stages of the legislative process. Aides draft legislation, negotiate with lobbyists, and plot strategy for floor action. Legislators are asked to debate and vote on a wide range of complex issues, and they need staff to provide the expertise that one person alone simply could not master.

Many members of Congress also view staff—especially large staffs—as a symbol of prestige and importance. To some members, the larger the staff, the more powerful a member appears. Similarly, many staffers feel that the more powerful the committee or member is that they work for, the more powerful they are.

Congress has more staff than any other national legislature. There are nearly twenty thousand aides who work directly for Congress and its 540 voting and nonvoting members (including the delegates from American Samoa, the District of Columbia, Guam, and the Virgin Islands, and the resident commissioner from Puerto Rico). By comparison, the Canadian parliament, with slightly more than four hundred senators and members of parliament, employs about 3,500 staff.[1]

Huge increases in the size of congressional staff came in two waves, after Congress reorganized itself in 1946 and 1970. As the size of staff increased, so did the costs of running Congress, which is now well over a billion-dollar enterprise. As recently as the mid-1960s, the cost of operating Congress was less than one-ninth of what it is today. Legislative branch appropriations, which include some nonlegislative activities, are nevertheless the best measure of its cost that Congress has provided over the years. That figure rose from more than $361 million in fiscal 1970 to more than $1.8 billion in fiscal 1990. The largest share goes to pay salaries.

Another ten thousand or so congressional employees are "support staff." They work for the Library of Congress, the General Accounting Office, or the other large agencies of the legislative branch. This chapter deals primarily with the two groups that work most directly with the members—personal staff and committee staff.

STAFFING PRACTICES

Senators and representatives were reluctant during the early years of Congress to admit that they

These five sisters worked as secretaries for members of Congress in the 1920s. Congressional employees today are drawn from a mix of backgrounds, but most are young, male, and well educated.

required staff assistance, either in the committees or in their own offices. According to William L. Morrow, in his book *Congressional Committees,* "Legislators were considered more erudite than most citizens and they believed any suggestion for staff assistance might be interpreted as a lack of confidence in their ability to master their jobs." [2]

Congressional staffing began as clerical assistance. In *Congressional Staffs,* Harrison W. Fox, Jr., and Susan Webb Hammond point out that to this day the account for paying personal staffers is still referred to as "clerk-hire." [3] Permanent, paid staffers were authorized first for committees. Until the 1820s and 1830s there were few standing committees, and members of committees handled committee matters without paid assistance. Congress rejected various requests to employ permanent committee clerks until about 1840 when, after

pleas by the chairmen, some clerical help was permitted in emergencies on a per diem or hourly basis. Funds for these part-time assistants were made available through special appropriations.

In 1856 the House Ways and Means and Senate Finance committees became the first to obtain regular appropriations for full-time clerks. Appropriations for other committees followed, but their staffing generally was limited to persons hired for housekeeping duties, such as stenographers and receptionists. Members or their personal aides (who were paid out of members' own pockets) usually handled substantive committee work and bill drafting. But the number of committee employees increased very gradually. By 1891 committee staff numbered only forty-one in the Senate and sixty-two in the House.

By the turn of the century, wrote George B.

Galloway, a specialist on Congress with the Library of Congress for many years, appropriations acts began to carry line items specifying funds for the standing committees of the House and Senate. The first comprehensive pay bill authorizing appropriations for all legislative employees, including committee clerks, was enacted in 1924. That act appropriated $270,100 for 141 Senate committee clerks and $200,490 for 120 House committee employees.

Senators were first authorized to hire personal aides in 1885, at a pay rate of six dollars a day. The House passed similar provisions in 1893. Before this time, members who were not committee chairmen either worked without personal assistance or they paid aides with personal funds.[4]

Committee staffs and personal office staffs were separated by an ill-defined line, both in practice and by statute. In the late nineteenth century, when chairmen had the authority to appoint clerks to assist with committee business, these clerks often worked on the chairman's district business as well. Debate on a clerk-hire bill in 1892 disclosed that some superfluous committees had been kept in existence under pressure from their chairmen, primarily so they would have the services of their committee clerks.

Distinctions between the duties of committee employees and members' personal staff remained blurred well into the twentieth century. Under provisions of the Legislative Pay Act of 1929, for example, when a senator assumed the chairmanship of a committee, the three senior clerks of his office staff became ex officio clerk and assistant clerks of that committee. Further, the act stipulated that the clerical staff of a Senate committee also would serve as secretarial workers for its chairman.

Congress tried in the Legislative Reorganization Act of 1946 to separate the roles of committee and personal staffs. That law stated that professional committee staff members "shall not engage in any work other than committee business, and no other duties may be assigned to them." Nonetheless, committee and subcommittee aides often handle personal and political work for the chairman of the panel to which they are attached.

Legislation passed in June 1975 further obscured the difference between the two types of staffers in the Senate. That measure allowed senators to hire up to three additional aides to help with committee duties. *(Details, p. 71)*

Staffing Reforms

Personal staffs did not increase much in size between the turn of the century and World War II. In 1946 representatives were authorized to employ five aides and the average Senate office had six staffers. Committee staffs also did not expand greatly; in 1943 there were 190 Senate committee aides and 114 in the House.[5]

As early as 1941, however, many in Congress realized that an overhaul of staffing procedures and the committee structure was necessary. Many members complained that an ever-increasing congressional workload placed a heavy burden on staff. As communications and transportation improved, voters could demand more from their elected officials. Consequently, casework increased. Furthermore, issues and legislation had become more complex. And ironically, because members wanted more staff help, more committees were created, which ultimately created more work.

Another problem that drove Congress to change its staffing practices was the lack of staff with technical expertise and skills. Congress relied on the executive branch and lobbying groups to provide specialized assistance and help with drafting bills. Members became concerned about an "executive branch dictatorship" and felt that Congress was becoming a second-class institution. This feeling was underscored by a warning issued to Congress in 1942 by President Franklin D. Roosevelt, who was frustrated with Congress's delay in enacting key administration proposals: "In the event that

House and Senate Support Offices

For its day-to-day operations, Congress is supported by the offices and staffs of the clerk of the House, the secretary of the Senate, the House and Senate sergeants at arms, the House doorkeeper, the House and Senate parliamentarians, and others.

The functions of the clerk of the House and the secretary of the Senate are administrative as well as quasi-judicial. The majority party elects both of the officials, who generally remain in their posts until that party loses control of the chamber (although each house retains the power to remove its officials).

The clerk and secretary perform a wide range of tasks. They process all legislation; prepare the daily digest and periodic reports for the *Congressional Record;* furnish stationery supplies, electrical and mechanical equipment, and office furniture; record and print bills and reports; disburse the payroll; compile lobby registration information; and supervise, respectively, the House and Senate libraries, the recording studios, the document rooms, property supply and repair services, and switchboards.

The House and Senate sergeants at arms do not wear uniforms but they are the police officers of their respective chambers. They attend all House and Senate floor sessions and are responsible for enforcing rules and maintaining decorum, ensuring the security of buildings and visitors, and appointing the Capitol police chief. In addition, the House sergeant at arms is in charge of the mace, a traditional symbol of legislative power and authority.

The House doorkeeper introduces the bearers of all messages, official guests, and members attending joint sessions. The doorkeeper is responsible for supervising doormen, pages, and barbers; issuing gallery passes; and performing a variety of custodial services. On the Senate side the sergeant at arms performs these functions.

The parliamentarians of the House and Senate sit in on all sessions to advise the presiding officers on parliamentary procedures. They help refer legislation to committees and they maintain compilations of the precedents of each chamber.

The House and Senate chaplains are officers of their respective chambers. The chaplains open each day's session with a prayer and provide other religious services to members, their families, and congressional staff.

The Office of the Senate Legal Counsel advises and represents senators, committees, officers, and staffers on legal matters relating to official Senate work and civil proceedings.

The House Office of the Law Revision Counsel develops and updates an official classification of U.S. laws. The office periodically prepares and publishes a new edition of the United States Code, including annual cumulative supplements of newly enacted laws.

Congress fails to act, and act adequately, I shall accept the responsibility, and I shall act." [6]

At that time, as the United States was entering World War II, Congress did not have the monetary resources to beef up its staff.

[In 1941], of every seven dollars it authorized the federal government to spend, Congress spent only one cent on itself. Its thirty-two- hundred-member staff was predominantly clerical and custodial, with not more than two hundred persons who could be considered legislative professionals. [Members] were often required to use their office clerks as the principal staff of any committee they chaired, thus ignoring professional competence as the foundation for committee staffing.

senators. They wanted to have, as Sen. Bob Packwood, R-Ore., stated, "the same access that the senior senators do to professional staff assistance." Senators were allowed to hire up to three staffers, called associate staff, depending on the type and number of committees a senator served on.

That change (S Res 60) was intended to prevent a senator who already had staff on a committee from getting more staff for that committee. Thus, it benefited primarily junior senators who had been excluded from separate staff on their committees because of their low-seniority status. The plan cut into the traditional power base that senior members enjoyed through their control of committee staff and was opposed by many of them for that reason.

The 1975 change also required senators to certify that their new aides worked only on committee business. But the funds to pay for the additional committee aides were merged with senators' general clerk-hire funds, thus allowing members to use the money as they wished. In addition, most associate staff work out of senators' personal offices and often are difficult to distinguish from the legislative assistants on senators' personal staffs.

Library of Congress

The entire staff of Sen. Harold H. Burton pose with the senator and Mrs. Burton in 1941. Total personal staff of senators increased from 590 in 1947 to 3,837 in 1989.

STAFF EXPLOSION

Congressional staffs expanded steadily following enactment of the 1946 Legislative Reorganization Act and they received another boost with the Legislative Reorganization Act of 1970. In 1947 there were 399 aides on House and Senate committees; by 1989 the number had jumped to 2,999—an increase of more than 650 percent. Similarly, in 1947 there were 2,030 House and Senate personal aides; in 1989 there were 11,406 personal staffers—an increase of more than 400 percent. *(Staff growth, table, p. 73)*

The post-World War II staff explosion came about for a variety of reasons: a desire for congressional independence from the executive branch, the increasing volume and complexity of legislative issues faced by Congress, competition among committees and their members, and an increase in mail and demands for services by constituents.

The continued growth of staff—especially committee staff—after the 1970 Legislative Reorganization Act can be linked to the reformist movement that swept Congress in the early 1970s. This time period was marked by the election of more activist members, the decline of the congressional seniority system, greater demands exerted by special interests, and a growing sense that junior and minority party members should get fairer treatment. House committee staffs were two and three-quarters times as large in 1979 as they were in 1970, and Senate committee staffs doubled over the same time period.[13]

The congressional-executive relationship also was a factor in staff growth during the 1970s. Before the mid-1960s Congress still depended to a large extent on the executive branch for information and advice on existing programs and legislative proposals. But distrust of the executive branch, partially the result of the Vietnam War and the Watergate scandal, led Congress to hire more and better qualified committee staff to monitor and evaluate executive branch performance and recommendations and to initiate more of its own legislation.

Also during the 1970s there was an explosion in the size of White House and executive office staff, by which Congress felt threatened. As the executive branch grew, Congress felt compelled to create its own bureaucracy to keep up. Sen. Daniel Patrick Moynihan, D-N.Y., termed this process the "Iron Law of Emulation." According to Moynihan, "Whenever any branch of government acquires a new technique which enhances its power in relation to the other branches, that technique will soon be adopted by those other branches as well." [14]

Similarly, the growth of lobby groups in Washington led to an increase in staff on Capitol Hill. Members needed more help to deal with the volume of special interest issues confronting them. Sen. James Abourezk, D-S.D., once argued that "an active, if sometimes redundant, congressional staff is imperative" to protect the public interest in the face of the often powerful "private constituencies that influence Congress."

Staff growth leveled off during the 1980s and early 1990s. Both personal staff and committee staff numbers have remained fairly stable. This trend may be attributed to the mood of fiscal austerity created by the budget deficit and the Gramm-Rudman-Hollings deficit reduction law.

Another factor in the slowdown of staff expansion was the effort begun by the Reagan administration in 1981 to shrink the federal government. The president's staff in the White House and

Executive Office of the President peaked at 5,721 in 1972; by 1988 the staff had dropped to 1,594. Although the number of White House staff had climbed to 1,717 in 1991 under President George Bush, it was still a far cry from the pre-1981 levels. [15]

Lawmakers—especially Republicans—echoed Reagan, calling for a reduction of the congressional bureaucracy. Both the House and Senate cut committee budgets 10 percent in 1981. The Republican-controlled Senate led the way, and the Democratic House felt pressured to follow suit.

Senate committee staffs underwent a one-shot 14 percent cut after the Republicans gained control in 1981 and promised to reverse the previous decade's trends. However, more than one-half of the cuts came from one committee, Judiciary. As significant as the cuts were, the Senate still had almost 60 percent more committee staff in 1989 than in 1970. [16]

Political considerations forced the House Democratic leadership in 1981 to combine investigative funds for all committees in a single package. Until then the House took up each committee's budget one at a time on the House floor. Under the Republican move to trim congressional budgets, Democrats feared that funds for some committees might suffer further cuts if each committee's request was considered individually.

Impact

So many aides have been recruited in recent years that the House and Senate have been forced to construct new office buildings as well as to convert former hotels, apartments, and federal buildings into temporary offices.

As Congress has grown, it has changed as an institution. What is most apparent is that the legislative branch has become more bureaucratic. With staff growth has come waste and duplication of effort. Some observers charge that many of the newer congressional aides are interested in little more than self-aggrandizement and getting their bosses reelected. They maintain that the availability of larger staffs is drawing Congress into areas where it has no business legislating. On the other hand, some Congress watchers argue that thanks to the larger congressional staff, lawmakers are better equipped to deal with complex and sensitive legislative issues.

Today's staffers are more highly qualified than ever before, and they come increasingly from professional rather than political backgrounds. As a result, Congress receives better information on which to base its decisions.

At the same time, some employees on Capitol Hill, especially those who have been there for a number of years, believe staffers often see their jobs merely as way stations on the road to other prospects. Once, legislative work was a career, even a cause; today, the place is often compared to a corporation or a big government bureaucracy—better managed than before, with many competent people working hard, but impersonal. As one staffer put it: "It used to be a way of life. Now it's a job."

Sarah M. Martin, a staffer on Capitol Hill for forty years, explained the change: "When I first started work here, you got to know everybody on the Hill. We were almost one family, really. We helped each other out, no matter what the party affiliation."

Now, she said, "It's more time-consuming. The bigness—especially with the subcommittees—has broken up the closeness between members and their personal staffs and the committee staffs. People are out to advance themselves, to prove their worth, rather than to find a career. There's a lot of selfish motivation."

As recently as the early 1970s, administration of the congressional bureaucracy was more informal. Before the Senate payroll was computerized in 1972, Senate staff were paid by lining up in front

Growth of Staff

Year	House Personal	House Committee	Senate Personal	Senate Committee
1891	n.a.	62	39	41
1914	n.a.	105	72	198
1930	870	112	280	163
1935	870	122	424	172
1947	1,440	193	590	290
1957	2,441	375	1,115	558
1967	4,055	589	1,749	621
1972	5,280	783	2,426	918
1976	6,939	1,548	3,251	1,534
1977	6,942	1,776	3,554	1,028
1978	6,944	1,844	3,268	1,151
1979	7,067	1,909	3,593	1,269
1980	7,371	1,917	3,746	1,191
1981	7,487	1,843	3,945	1,022
1982	7,511	1,839	4,041	1,047
1983	7,606	1,970	4,059	1,075
1984	7,385	1,944	3,949	1,095
1985	7,528	2,009	4,097	1,080
1986	7,920*	1,954	3,774*	1,075
1987	7,584	2,024	4,075	1,074
1988	7,564	1,976	3,977	970
1989	7,569	1,986	3,837	1,013

n.a. = not available

* Senate figures reflect the period immediately after Gramm-Rudman mandated staffing cuts. House figures are for the entire fiscal year, thus averaging post-Gramm-Rudman staffing levels with previous, higher levels.

Note: Figures for 1977-1989 committee staff are for the statutory and investigative staffs of standing committees. They do not include select committee staffs.

Sources: For 1891 through 1976, Harrison W. Fox, Jr., and Susan W. Hammond, Congressional Staffs: The Invisible Force in American Lawmaking (New York: The Free Press, 1977), 171. For 1977 through 1989, Norman J. Ornstein, Thomas E. Mann, and Michael J. Malbin, Vital Statistics on Congress, 1991-1992 (Washington, D.C.: Congressional Quarterly, 1992), 126, 130.

of the Disbursing Office, where each employee was handed an envelope stuffed with his or her pay in cash. "You didn't even have to give them your name," recalled Chester Smith, a retired staff member of the Senate Rules Committee, who went to work on the Hill in 1946. "They knew who you

were by your face. Now the pay-line would go all
the way down to the Potomac [River] and back."

Effects of Committee Staff Expansion.

The effect of committee staff expansion
was predictable—personnel costs have ballooned.
In fiscal year 1960, approximately $12.3 million
was appropriated for permanent committee staff
and investigations staff in both the House and
Senate. By fiscal 1984 the amount was more than
$128.4 million.[17]

Another result was, not surprisingly, an increase
in the volume of legislation considered by committees. While more employees were hired to deal
with the increasing workload facing committee
members, the additional staff created more work,
necessitating still more staff. Many aides were
policy initiators, pushing for certain reforms they
personally favored. Others were encouraged by the
members who hired them to dig up issues that the
lawmakers could use to draw attention to themselves, in the media or back home in their own
constituencies.

Although some indicators of the congressional
workload—the number of bills introduced, reported,
and passed; the number of votes taken; and the
number of subcommittee and committee meetings—
have decreased in the past decade, workload is still
quite heavy. Congress now passes more omnibus
bills, which contain many separate bills rolled into
one big package. Confirmation hearings that in-
tensely scrutinize a nominee, such as those for John
Tower and Robert Bork, have been especially time-
consuming in the past few years, as have congressional and executive ethics investigations. In addition, the budget deficit has curtailed members from
introducing or considering legislation that will cost a
lot of money; many members now concentrate their
legislative efforts on low-cost, yet politically visible,
issues, such as a constitutional amendment banning
flag burning. However, the role of staff in all of
these efforts is just as important as in the regular

legislative work they do.

One of the most important changes that resulted
from the growth of committee staff was the emphasis on subcommittee government—and the growth
of subcommittee staff. This was especially true in
the House, which diffused committee power in the
1970s reforms it passed.

In 1973 the House Democratic Caucus adopted
a "subcommittee bill of rights" stating that a
majority caucus within each committee would determine subcommittee chairmen, jurisdictions, and
budgets. In a 1974 committee reorganization plan,
the House required all committees with more than
fifteen members to establish at least four subcommittees; the threshold committee size was
changed to twenty members by the House Democratic Caucus in 1975. This move was significant
because it institutionalized subcommittees in the
House for the first time.

As the power of subcommittees grew so did their
staffs. By the late 1970s the number of staffers
working for subcommittees equaled the number
assigned to full committees in the 1960s.

A further change in House practices adopted in
1975 affected subcommittee staff growth. The new
rule allowed subcommittee chairmen and the highest ranking minority member on each panel to hire
one staff person each to work directly for them on
their subcommittee business.

Where House subcommittee staff grew by
nearly 650 percent in the 1970s, Senate subcommittee staff grew by less than 50 percent. In
1979 just two committees, Judiciary and Governmental Affairs, employed nearly three-fourths of
the Senate's subcommittee staff. Several committees
do not even have subcommittees. Senate subcommittee staff did not grow so quickly because the
Senate retained far more centralized staffing arrangements than the House.

Effects of Personal Staff Expansion.

The expansion of personal staffs has meant a tremendous increase in the amount of money it takes to run a member's office. In 1970 each representative was entitled to an annual clerk-hire allowance of $149,292 for a staff not to exceed fifteen employees for a district under five hundred thousand persons, or $157,092 for a staff not to exceed sixteen employees for a member representing a larger district. In 1979 the annual clerk-hire allowance for a staff of twenty-two employees was $288,156; by 1991 the allowance for the same number of staff rose to $475,000.[18]

Senators' staffing allowances have similarly increased. In 1970 the clerk-hire allowance ranged from $239,805 to $401,865 (the allowance varies according to state population). In 1979 the range was from $508,221 to $1,021,167, and by this time most senators had an additional legislative assistance allowance of $157,626. By 1991 the clerk-hire allowance jumped to a range of $814,000 to $1,760,000; the legislative assistance allowance was $269,000.[19]

The modern congressional office more closely resembles a large company customer service department than the typical legislative office of an earlier period. Until World War I, a single clerk handled a member's entire correspondence. In those days, congressional mail usually involved awarding rural mail routes, arranging for Spanish-American War pensions, sending out free seeds and, occasionally, explaining legislation.[20]

House Postmaster Robert V. Rota has testified that the volume of incoming mail has skyrocketed over the past two decades. "Since I was elected as postmaster in 1972, the volume of incoming mail [in the House] has increased more than five-fold. . . . To process the mail received by the House of Representatives, we operate twenty-one hours a day. . . . Mail deliveries are received every hour on the hour."[21]

The demand for services—usually assistance with a constituent's problems with federal agencies—has increased as government has become more involved in the daily lives of Americans. But members also have helped to stimulate constituent demands. They have expanded use of mobile offices, radio programs, and newsletters to advertise the availability of their services and to garner political support.

The emphasis on constituent services is shown by the increase in personal staff working in a member's district or state office. In 1990 more than 41 percent of a representative's staff worked in a district office—up from 22.5 percent in 1972. Thirty-five percent of a senator's staff worked in a state office in 1990, as opposed to only 12.5 percent in 1972.[22] Members contend that large staffs are necessary to serve constituents as well as to properly carry out government oversight, which, it is argued, often saves taxpayers' money in the long run through better surveillance of the administration of the laws.

Assistants or Policy Makers?

Congress's growing dependence on staff has enhanced the power of staff—the so-called unelected representatives. Some observers find this disturbing. As senators and representatives spend more and more time raising money for their reelection campaigns, they delegate more and more work to staff professionals, most of whom have advanced degrees and considerable experience and come to Capitol Hill ready to make substantive policy decisions. The extent of that influence is under continuing debate.

In his book *The Power Game,* journalist Hedrick Smith quotes several members of Congress who agreed they were highly dependent on their aides. Said House majority whip Tony Coelho, D-Calif., in 1986: "When I leave a meeting, I don't have time to do the follow up. . . . The staff controls that meeting, that issue. I don't have time to make phone calls, to listen to the lobbyists. What is power? Information. Follow-through. Drafting an op-ed article."

R. Michael Jenkins

Shortly after becoming Speaker of the House in 1989, Thomas S. Foley, D-Wash., held this informal staff meeting to discuss the legislative schedule. Seated at Foley's left is Heather Foley, his wife and unpaid chief of staff.

Smith quotes some senators as bemoaning the trend toward communication through aides. From Sen. William S. Cohen, R-Maine: "More and more you are dependent on your staff. There is so much competition among staffs, fighting over issues, that sometimes you'll call a senator and ask, 'Why are you opposing me on this?' and he'll say, 'I didn't know I was.' And you'll say, "Well, check with your staff and see.' "

From Sen. Ernest F. Hollings, D-S.C.: "There are many senators who felt that all they were doing is running around and responding to the staff: my staff fighting with your staff, your staff competing with mine. . . . It is sad. I heard a senator the other day tell me another senator hadn't been in his office for three years; it is just staff. Everybody is working for the staff, staff, staff, driving you nutty, in fact. It has gotten to the point where the senators never actually sit down and exchange ideas and learn from the experience of others and listen. Now it is how many nutty whiz kids you get on the staff, to get you magazine articles and get you headlines and get all of these other things done." [23]

Others feel that the influence of congressional staff is exaggerated. After Senate Majority Leader Howard H. Baker, Jr., R-Tenn., retired from Congress and joined a Washington law firm, he said he was amazed that lobbyists paid so much attention to staff aides; he felt that much of the real work of the Senate was done by individual senators:

"I was struck by the fact that [lobbyists] had list after list of people on the staff they'd gone to see. . . . That's a side of Washington I hadn't clearly seen while I was in the Senate. I was surprised it was almost the total focus of this little group. . . . I think part of it is an illusion. . . . Because, you know, when I met with most committee chairmen every Tuesday morning around the conference table in my office, I saw how it worked. They would really go at it hammer and tongs on particular items within their jurisdiction. So I think the impact of staff is overrated. But God knows, there's enough of them, they generate enough memos, and I know they attract lobbyists and lawyers like flies." [24]

But some observers see positive results in the empowerment of staff. By initiating policy, the staffs help Congress retain its vitality and independence from the executive branch. According to political scientist Malbin: "Most other national legislatures do not give individual members similar staff resources; most legislatures depend on their cabinets for almost all policy initiatives. Congress is not so passive today, thanks largely to its staff." [25]

COMMITTEE STAFF

While congressional committees vary in their organization, most have dual staffs—one professional and one clerical. These generally are headed by a staff director and a chief clerk, respectively. Although the distinctions between the professional and clerical staffs are blurred on many committees, the duties of each can be separated roughly.

The clerical staff is responsible for the day-to-day running of the committee and assisting the members and professional staff. Some of its routine tasks include: keeping the committee calendar up to date, processing committee publications, referring bills that have been introduced to the appropriate departments and administration officials for comment, preparing the bill dockets, maintaining files, performing stenographic work, announcing hearings and contacting witnesses, and opening and sorting mail.

Professional staff members handle committee policy and legislative matters generally, including legal and other types of research, public relations, statistical and other technical work, and drafting and redrafting legislative language and amendments. *(Functions of committee staff, p. 78)*

The clerical and professional aides just described are a committee's statutory, or permanent, staff. Their positions are established by rules of the House or Senate or by law and are funded annually in the legislative branch appropriations bill. Committees also hire additional personnel for investigative work. These employees are considered temporary, but they often remain with the committees for extended periods.

In the House, funds for investigative staff are approved separately from statutory staff funds. The Senate in 1981 eliminated the distinction between the two types for funding purposes. This was done to gain better financial control over soaring staff costs. Senate committees now submit all funding requests in one budget document to the Rules and Administration Committee for review.

Generally, House committees are entitled to thirty staffers paid out of statutory funds. Most of the committees put their highest-paid staff in this category and not under the investigative budget, which is reviewed by the House Administration Committee. Over the years, investigative employees have accounted for much of the increase in committee staff costs, as the budgets for these aides are flexible. In addition to staff salaries, House investigative budgets include money for office equipment, consultants, publications, and for travel within the United States.

House investigative budgets do not include the money the committees get for hiring statutory staff or for printing expenses, stenographic costs, foreign travel, stationery, and some communications expenses. The investigative total also does not include funding for the House Appropriations or Budget committees, both of which are included directly in the annual legislative appropriations bill and are not limited to thirty statutory staffers.

Committees seeking additional investigative help also may use the services of legislative or executive branch agencies. The congressional General Accounting Office, the Treasury Department, and the FBI, among others, frequently are called upon for assistance.

Functions

While staff responsibilities and influence vary from one committee to another, the following list includes the important functions performed by aides on almost all House and Senate committees:

Planning Agendas. Staffers work with chairmen to plan committee agendas, decide which issues to consider, schedule hearings and markups, and plan floor action.

Organizing Hearings. Staffers set up hearings on legislation and issues of interest to the committee leadership as well as on annual or periodic authorization measures on which the panel has jurisdiction. Aides select witnesses, prepare questions, inform the press, brief committee members, and occasionally substitute for members or the chairman if they cannot attend hearings. In many instances a member will prepare a list of questions for aides to ask witnesses if he or she cannot be present. Even when the chairman is present, senior aides with special knowledge sometimes are asked to question witnesses on technical subjects.

Oversight and Investigations. Much original research is conducted by staff members on issues that come before a committee. This usually involves a critique of existing legislation, court decisions, and current practices. Aides on the Armed Services and foreign policy committees, for example, often travel to areas under consideration by the committee. Sometimes staffers hold regional hearings to get opinions from citizens interested in a particular bill or subject.

Bill Markup and Amendment Drafting. Staff aides assist in marking up bills by explaining technical provisions, outlining policy questions, analyzing proposed changes following committee decisions, and incorporating the decisions in successive revisions of the bill. Although staff members may assist in writing or rewriting proposed bills and amendments, they often serve as liaison between the Office of the Legislative Counsel (there is an office for each chamber), committee members, government agencies, and special interest groups during the drafting of legislation.

Preparing Reports. Committee reports that accompany bills sent to the full chamber are almost entirely staff products. Often, the reports are the only reference available to noncommittee members when a bill is considered by the House or Senate. Staff aides consult with the chairman or the majority party members to decide what should be emphasized in the report. Minority party members and opponents of the bill in question often may file "minority views," which as a rule are drafted by the committee's minority staff members. Then the staff writes the report, usually conforming to a standard format. Reports generally include three basic ingredients—the main body, which explains the bill and gives background and interpretation; the section-by-section analysis of the provisions of the bill; and a written comparison of the bill with existing law.

Preparing for Floor Action. The top committee aides, those most familiar with the legislation, often accompany the committee chairman, or the bill's sponsor or manager if not the chairman, when the bill is debated on the floor. They may be needed particularly to assist in formulating amendments to the bill or amendments to counter those introduced by other members in the chamber.

Conference Committee Work. The staffs of corresponding committees in each chamber work together on the preparation of conference reports and in resolving differences in legislation initially

Ken Heinen

Staff members stand by as Rep. John D. Dingell, D-Mich., chairman of the House Energy and Commerce Committee, confers with a committee member. Staffers cannot vote, but their imprint is on every other step in the legislative process.

considered by those committees and subsequently passed by the House and Senate.

Liaison with Executive Branch, Special Interests. Staff aides communicate frequently with executive branch officials and lobbyists on legislative proposals before the committee. Some members regard this activity as the most consequential of all staff work. Rep. Bob Eckhardt, D-Texas, said in 1969: "The key point of contact is usually between a highly specialized lobbyist and the specialized staff people of a standing committee. Intimate friendships spring up there—it's the rivet point. Friendships that last terms. They probably have a greater influence on legislation, especially if it's technical." Lobbyists and representatives of special interest groups, particularly those that have Washington offices, often provide staff aides with detailed information and answers to questions.

Press Relations. Committee staff perform a number of press-related tasks. They alert reporters to upcoming hearings, markup sessions, and floor action on committee-reported measures. Aides answer questions from the press and public, provide background information on legislation before the committee and on recent committee decisions on legislation, and write press releases. In addition, they make committee members accessible to the media and generally work to obtain favorable publicity for the committee.

Recruitment and Tenure

Most committee employees are selected by the chairman, or the top-ranking minority party member, as a perquisite of office, subject only to nominal approval by the full committee.

From surveys and interviews with committee

staff, one can make some generalizations about today's professional aides (as distinct from clerical aides). They are relatively young and most are male. Most committee professionals are residents of the District of Columbia metropolitan area, in contrast to members' personal office staff. The majority of the aides have advanced degrees, particularly law degrees, and many bring previous experience in the executive branch to their committee positions.[26] Susan Webb Hammond has observed a recent trend toward career development in committee staff positions, especially considering the level of experience and expertise required of most committee staffers.[27]

The tenure of committee employees is subject to the chairman or member who hired them, and aides can be fired with or without cause. Congressional aides do not need to be reminded about the precarious nature of committee employment. As one Capitol Hill observer pointed out, "Staff members all have friends whose chairman retired, switched committees, or was beaten, leaving them with a new chairman wanting to 'clean house.' They all know competent people who were fired without warning because the boss sensed a slight, or just felt it was time for a change." [28]

The power to fire congressional staff gives members significant control over individuals to whom they have delegated great responsibility. Members of Congress can instantly demote or dismiss a staffer they feel has exceeded their authority.

Salaries and Benefits

Salaries of committee employees increased dramatically in the decades after World War II. In 1945 House employees were listed under "clerk-hire" categories with annual base pay of $2,500. The 1970 Legislative Reorganization Act converted the "base pay" system of the House into a monthly salary system and raised the compensation levels of committee employees. The highest-paid committee aides in the House received an annual salary in 1991 of approximately $115,092; in the Senate, $99,215.

Both the House and the Senate are required by law to report on salaries, allowances, and expenses paid to members and members' personal and committee staffs. The "Report of the Clerk of the House" is issued quarterly; the "Report of the Secretary of the Senate," every six months. (Both reports are available to the public through the House and Senate Document rooms.)

Committee staff receive the same cost-of-living increases and insurance and retirement benefits as do other Capitol Hill employees. Vacation and sick leave policies vary according to committee.

Partisanship and Minority Staffing

Partisanship of committee employees has been and remains a controversial topic. For many years the chairman's prerogative prevailed in the selection of staff members. Thus, most of the employees were from the majority party.

The 1946 Legislative Reorganization Act omitted any provision for apportioning the professional staff of a committee between the chairman and the ranking minority member. The act simply stated that "staff members shall be assigned to the chairman and ranking minority member of such committee as the committee may deem advisable." Committees interpreted that provision in various ways, and the whim of the chairman often determined the number of minority aides hired.

In the 1960s Republicans began to press for formally recognized and permanently authorized minority staffing on all committees. Columnist Roscoe Drummond, writing in 1961, advanced the Republicans' arguments:

If the Republican members of Congress are ever to be in a position to clarify, expound, and defend their stand on the major issues ... and to advance constructive alternatives of their own, they must get a steady flow of adequate, reliable, competent research and information from an adequate, reliable, and competent professional staff. This staff must be in the service of the minority, selected by the minority, and working for it.[29]

Another problem facing minority staff is inequitable treatment. Sometimes minority staff are paid less than their counterparts working for the majority, and minority senators and representatives often must wait longer than majority members to appoint staff.[30]

Several changes were made in minority staffing in the 1970s. The 1970 Legislative Reorganization Act provided that at least three full-time minority staff aides were to be assigned to most committees of the House and Senate.

House. In January 1971 the House voted to delete the provisions of the 1970 Legislative Reorganization Act providing that one-third of committee investigative funds—used to hire part-time professionals and to assist members—be allocated to the minority side. The Democratic Caucus had voted to bind all House Democrats to vote for the deletion, a move that angered Republicans and revealed clearly the importance members attach to the issue of congressional staffing.

The minority staffing issue surfaced again in late 1974, as representatives debated a proposal to reorganize House committees. That plan called for giving Republicans ten of thirty staff members assigned to committees by statute and one-third of the investigative staff allotted to subcommittees by the House Administration Committee. But when the Democratic Caucus met in January 1975, a resolution was introduced to nullify the one-third minority investigative staff guarantee. The caucus agreed to a compromise that allowed subcommittee

chairmen and top-ranking minority members to hire one staff person each to work on their subcommittees—up to a maximum of six subcommittees—but dropped the one-third minority investigative staff guarantee. House rules permitted standing committees a total of six subcommittees. Although the staff increase applied specifically to subcommittees, the revision was widely billed as an increase of twelve in the number of statutory committee employees. The actual number of committee employees permitted by statute remained at thirty.

The minority staffing compromise produced one of the most significant changes of the many revisions made in House rules during the 1970-75 period. Incorporated into the rules January 14, 1975, the compromise was seen as crucial to strengthening the subcommittees and giving House minority members a meaningful opportunity to influence legislation. In general, dispersing power among committee members and reducing the authority of House committee chairmen also meant a dispersal of control over committee staffs and budgets.

The idea of allocating one-third of investigative staff to the minority came up again in 1989. This time House Democrats agreed to let the minority have at least 20 percent of committee investigative staff positions, with an eventual goal of 33 percent. Although only 19 percent of the investigative staff positions were allocated to the minority in 1990, most Republicans agreed that progress was being made toward more equitable staffing and that the real problem was a shortage of funds for expansion.

Senate. As part of the Senate's 1975 change in committee staffing (S Res 60), all minority members were authorized to hire up to three personal committee aides.

In 1977 the Senate directed that committee staffs should be allocated in proportion to the number of majority and minority members on a standing committee. The measure further specified that a "majority of the minority members of any committee may, by resolution, request that at least one-third of the funds of the committee for statutory, investigative, and clerical personnel ... be allocated to the minority members."

Majority-Minority Staff Cooperation. The degree of cooperation between the majority and minority staffs varies with each committee. It is difficult to be nonpartisan on Capitol Hill, and most staffers have party or philosophical preferences. Even more important, most staffers work for a single member or the majority or minority committee leadership and must act in accordance with their wishes. A few committees, however— Appropriations, ethics, and the Joint Committee on Taxation, among others—have traditions of professional nonpartisan staffing.

From the late 1940s to the late 1970s, the Senate Foreign Relations Committee had a bipartisan staff that served all committee members regardless of party or seniority. In 1979, however, a group of Republican senators led by Jesse Helms of North Carolina, S. I. Hayakawa of California, and Richard G. Lugar of Indiana, requested and received separate minority staff. In 1981, when Republicans took control of the Senate, the partisan staffing arrangement continued.

The benefits of a nonpartisan system are evident in the case of the Joint Tax Committee staff, maintains Michael Malbin, who studied the committee in the late 1970s. These aides serve as the principal staff on tax legislation for both the House Ways and Means and Senate Finance committees. On all major issues likely to be considered by the two committees on tax-related measures, the joint committee aides, according to Malbin, outline the political interests of both major parties. This information then is published before the committees meet so that all members of the House and Senate,

the press, and the public can understand the issues and political implications before the committee begins its work.[31]

Jeffrey H. Birnbaum and Alan S. Murray, who followed the passage of the 1986 Tax Reform Act in their book, *Showdown at Gucci Gulch,* described the Joint Tax Committee in action, showing how important its nonpartisan staff are:

> [The staff of the joint committee] were not beholden to any single member. Their job was not political, and their bosses were many.... [They] served as a reservoir of inhouse expertise for the entire Congress, especially the two tax-writing committees. Joint Tax aides shaped and analyzed every change in tax law proposed by their bosses and often came up with suggestions themselves. Their revenue estimates on the changes were gospel. In tax reform, an exercise driven by revenue estimates and income-distribution charts, Joint Tax pronouncements were crucial.[32]

PERSONAL STAFF

Personal staffs are set up differently in each congressional office. Whether a representative or senator chooses to emphasize constituent service or legislation probably makes the biggest difference in how the office is organized. A member's personality is another factor.

Most congressional offices have an administrative assistant (AA), legislative assistants (LA's), caseworkers, and at least one press secretary. Many also have an office manager, appointments secretary, legislative correspondent, and systems or computer manager.

The administrative assistant, sometimes called the executive assistant, often serves as the member's alter ego and directs and supervises the office.

Teresa Zabala

Rep. Peter J. Visclosky, D-Ind., left, works with his executive assistant, Sarah Wells Duffy, in this 1985 picture. Duffy previously was a Washington lobbyist for the American Psychological Association.

Frequently, the AA serves as the member's chief political adviser, keeping the member abreast of district and Capitol Hill politics. The AA usually is in charge of the staff, or shares these supervisory responsibilities with the staff who manage the legislative staff, clerical staff, and staff in the state or district offices.

Functions

In the modern Congress, no senator or representative tries to "go it alone." Some are more inclined than others to try to "micromanage" their affairs, but in general members depend on staff to handle the nuts-and-bolts work of a congressional office. Reliance on staff is underscored by this picture of a member's typical day:

On a normal day, a senator or [representative] has two and sometimes three simultaneous committee hearings, floor votes, issues caucuses, meetings with other congressmen from his state or region, plus lobbyists, constituents, and press to handle. He will dart into one hearing, get a quick fill-in from his staffer, inject his ten minutes' worth and rush on to the next event, often told by an aide how to vote as he rushes onto the floor. Only the staff specialist has any continuity with substance. The member is constantly hop-scotching.[33]

Constituent Service. A major responsibility of personal staffs, especially in the House, is service to the people back in the state or district. Staffers respond to a myriad of constituent requests—they untangle bureaucratic snarls in collecting Social Security or veterans' benefits; they answer questions about student loans and similar programs; they help home state or district organizations to navigate red tape for landing federal grants; they respond to constituent mail on legislative and national issues; and they produce newsletters and other mailings to keep constituents informed of their representative's or senator's activities.

Such services are important not only for the benefits they provide to constituents, but also for the relationship they help to foster between a member of Congress and a voter. Former congressional staffer Mark Bisnow says that

> [constituent service] is often considered one of the more beneficial things congressmen do, but the motivation goes beyond mere charity; personal touches typically matter to voters as much as larger issues of ideology, voting record, or even public reputation. As a result, constituents occupy almost deified status in the eyes of Hill offices, a flotilla of paid aides poised to handle their problems. Too bad for a challenger who can do nothing more than walk the district at his own expense.[34]

Junior members of Congress tend to focus more attention on constituent services than more senior members do, and House members spend more time on casework than do senators. In both chambers, however, senior legislators apparently receive pro-portionately more casework requests than do junior members, possibly because senior members are considered more powerful and better equipped to resolve constituents' problems.[35]

Caseworkers may be called research assistants or staff assistants. Their operations may be centered in either the member's Washington office, or the state/district office.

Legislation. The making of laws is the fundamental job of a member of Congress. To do the work, members need legislative assistants for substantive and political guidance through the daily congressional agenda of complex, interdependent issues. There are more committee meetings than a member can adequately prepare for. Other members, federal officials, special interest groups, and sometimes even the White House staff must be consulted before final decisions are made, and often there are lengthy floor debates going well into the evening. A member must rely heavily on staff at every major phase of the legislative process.

Congressional offices have one or more legislative assistants who work with the senator or representative on the member's committees and help to draft bills and amendments and recommend policy initiatives and alternatives. LA's also monitor committee sessions that the member cannot attend and they may write the lawmaker's speeches and prepare position papers. In many offices, LA's are supervised by a legislative director—normally the senior legislative assistant.

In Senate offices, where there are more staffers, a team of LA's in an office often will divide up and specialize in various issues. In the House, one or two LA's alone may handle legislation for the member, or, in some cases, the member delegates the handling of legislative correspondence and personally takes care of monitoring active legislation.

Other Duties. Personal staffers handle other chores besides casework and legislation. The press secretary serves as the member's chief spokesperson to the news media. Press aides compose news releases dealing with legislative issues as well as notable casework or grants efforts, write newsletters, and organize press conferences. Because they deal almost exclusively with hometown media outlets, some House press aides are based in the district offices rather than in Washington. Where there is no press secretary, press relations are handled by the AA or a legislative assistant. Senators, who receive more national publicity and represent larger areas, often have several deputy press secretaries or assistant press staff.

The office manager, who often is the second-level manager in a congressional office, is in charge of handling clerical and computer systems functions.

The appointments secretary, who also may be called an executive secretary or a scheduler, normally handles personal appointments and travel arrangements for the member. An executive secretary who has been in a member's office for some time often exercises indirect, if not direct, control over other staff members.

A legislative correspondent drafts responses to letters concerning pending legislation. In some offices, the LA may draft letters in a particular subject area; in others, the legislative correspondent drafts letters for the LA's regardless of the subject.

The systems manager coordinates the member's correspondence management system (CMS) operations, which produces form letters. With the enormous amount of mail members of Congress receive each year, CMS operations have become an important function.

Personal staff members also play an important role in the reelection campaigns of their member. They may compile mailing lists, organize fund—raisers, and, in the Senate, solicit campaign contributions.

Relations with Committee Staff. Besides the help they get from personal aides, senior senators and representatives are assisted on legislative matters by staffs of the committees and subcommittees on which they serve. In addition, all senators since 1975 have been authorized up to three aides to help with their committee business. The chairman of a standing committee actually has two staffs. It is not unusual for an aide to do both committee work and personal casework for a member, no matter which payroll he or she is on. *(Committee staff structure, p. 77)*

Recruitment and Tenure

Personal aides are hired by the individual representative or senator. Although there are House and Senate employment offices, most hiring is based on informal contacts—who knows whom. Potential staffers may seek out members who are involved in particular issue areas, who are known to pay well, who are from a certain area of the country, or who have a particular ideological bent. Conversely, members may hire staffers for some of the same reasons.[36]

A major question for members is whether to hire from the state or district, or to go outside for persons with more experience. This is especially a problem for first-term representatives and senators who may not have many Washington contacts and who feel indebted to their campaign staff. As freshmen, these members may feel it is especially important to cultivate state and district contacts. A staffer who came to Washington with the then newly elected senator Pete Domenici, R-N.M., said he soon realized how important it is to strike a balance when hiring staff:

> We had a lot of people we felt we had to hire from the campaign. We brought a lot of them with us. . . . The big mistake we made was that we did not hire anyone who knew the

Senate. . . . I had to check ten offices every time I wanted to find out how you did something. It was insane.[37]

The party loyalty of staff is a "secondary consideration" to most representatives and senators when making hiring decisions. "It may be [that members] consider their aides already self-screened: If someone wants to work for them, their politics must be compatible." [38]

Members are entitled to money from a clerk-hire allowance to run and staff their office. The clerk-hire money is divided equally among representatives. For senators, the money is divided according to the state's population. (Details on clerk-hire allowance, see Salaries and Benefits section, below)

The characteristics of personal staff vary greatly from those of committee staff. A vivid picture of personal aides was painted by a former House legislative assistant:

House LA's tend to be young, commonly in their twenties; theirs can be an entry-level professional position requiring no previous Hill experience. (Committee staffers, in contrast, tend to be more specialized, and therefore older and of greater experience.) Their workaday world is informal and often frenetic. . . . Fifty-to-sixty hour work weeks are not unusual. Under constant time pressure and a multitude of urgent assignments, LA's typically switch among projects and topics by the half hour; they learn to write quickly, think politically, and argue combatively. In crowded offices, their desks nudged up against each other in ways that would affront a fire marshal, they do their own typing, photocopying, and phone-calling. They then suspend any calm reflections until things settle down again at six or seven or eight o'clock at night. . . .[39]

Like committee staff, personal staffers have little or no job security. Their tenure is up to the member who hired them. Neither personal nor committee staffers are protected under most labor laws that apply to other federal employees, a fact that earned Congress the nickname, "The Last Plantation."

Salaries and Benefits

There are few regulations to guide members in setting pay rates for their personal aides. Salaries for personal staff in both the House and Senate are drawn from a clerk-hire allowance. The Senate also has a separate fund for legislative assistance. (House and Senate allowances, p. 87)

Each House member is limited to a certain number of employees: eighteen full-time and four part-time. There is no limit in the Senate.

There are ceilings on pay levels—in 1991 personal staff in the House could earn up to $101,331 annually; the Senate figure was approximately $120,000. And there is a minimum pay level—1991 levels were $1,200 per year in the House and $1,530 in the Senate—but these salaries are normally for interns. The House also is regulated by minimum wage laws; the minimum wage in 1991 was $4.25 per hour.

But setting salaries and benefits for personal staff is left to the discretion of each member of Congress. Similar jobs in different offices may command very different salaries. Formal policies on working hours, vacation time, sick leave, and maternity leave do not necessarily exist and vary from office to office. The House passed legislation in 1989 to bring its employees under the protections of the Fair Labor Standards Act, which means that House offices may have to provide overtime pay for certain employees and written job descriptions. However, as of mid-1991 the House Administration Committee had yet to issue guidelines on how to implement the act. And once the guidelines were issued, it seemed likely that how the act was implemented would be left up to the discretion of each House office.

Most House and Senate employees qualify for annual cost-of-living adjustments (COLAs), which also are given to federal employees. Beginning January 1, 1992, COLAs for members of Congress and staff were to be calculated by subtracting 0.5 percent from the previous year's Economic Cost Index, which measures inflation of private industry salaries. A ceiling on COLAs was set at 5 percent.

However, the additional cost-of-living funds are not automatically included in congressional staffers' paychecks. Instead, they are added to the members' committee and personal payroll funds. A member or committee chairman can choose to give his employees the increase, use the money to hire more staffers, or return the money to the Treasury at the end of the year.

The salaries of some congressional staff—such as the clerk of the House, secretary of the Senate, the parliamentarians, House counsel, and legislative counsel—are statutory. This means their salaries (and raises) are funded by legislative appropriations and, like senators and representatives, their raises and cost-of-living increases are guaranteed.

House Allowance. In 1991 the clerk-hire allowance of each House member was $475,000 a year, which members could use to hire up to eighteen full-time and four temporary aides in their Washington and district offices. That allowance represented an increase of $236,420 since 1977. The increase in the staff allowance mainly has benefited junior members, who do not have the committee staff assistance enjoyed by their senior colleagues.

A maximum of $50,000 from a representative's clerk-hire allowance can be transferred to his official expenses allowance for use in other categories, such as computer and related services. In addition, a House member may allocate up to $50,000 from the official expenses allowance to supplement the clerk-hire allowance, provided that monthly clerk-hire disbursements do not exceed 10 percent of the total clerk-hire allowance. *(Official expenses allowances, p. 43)*

Before 1979 the maximum number of personal aides a representative could hire was eighteen, with no exceptions. In July of that year the House approved a rules change permitting members to add up to four more staffers to their payrolls—without counting them toward the ceiling of eighteen—if their jobs fit into one of five categories:

- A part-time employee, defined as one who does not work more than fifteen full working days a month or who is paid $1,270 a month or less.
- A "shared" employee—an employee, such as a computer expert, who is on the payroll of two or more members simultaneously.
- An intern in the member's Washington office, defined as an employee hired for up to 120 days and paid $1,160 a month or less.
- A temporary employee, defined as a staff member hired for three months or less and assigned a specific task or function.
- A person who temporarily replaces an employee on leave without pay.

In 1976 the House Administration Committee instituted a series of reforms governing staff allowances in the aftermath of the sex-payroll scandal that forced Rep. Wayne L. Hays, D-Ohio, to resign as chairman of the committee. At the same time, the House stripped the committee of its unilateral power to alter representatives' benefits and allowances.

The committee's reforms required all representatives, including chairmen of committees and subcommittees, to certify monthly the salaries and duties of their staff and to disclose any kinships between staff employees and any House member. Quarterly reports detailing how House allowances are spent were required for the first time. The reports of the clerk of the House are indexed by the name of the employee and by the member or House officer employing the person, showing the employee's title and salary.

The House allowed its Administration Committee, without further action by the full chamber, to adjust the clerk-hire allowance to reflect federal government cost-of-living raises.

Senate Allowance. The clerk-hire allowance of senators varies with the size of the member's state. For 1991 the annual allowance ranged from $814,000 for states with a population of fewer than 1 million residents to $1,760,000 for states with more than 28 million.

Senators may hire as many aides as they wish within their allowance; typically, this ranges between twenty-five and sixty, depending on the size of the state and the salary level.

The Senate clerk-hire allowance has remained essentially unchanged since 1968, aside from annual cost-of-living adjustments and additional staff funds provided to some senators as a result of a 1975 Senate rules change authorizing junior members to hire committee aides.

Under the 1975 action, senators were allotted a separate allowance to appoint up to three additional staffers to do specialized work on a senator's committees. The fiscal 1978 appropriations bill for the legislative branch combined this additional committee assistance allowance with senators' administrative and clerical allowance, so the annual Senate clerk-hire allowance actually consisted of two separate allowances. In 1991 each senator was authorized $269,000 for legislative assistance in addition to the regular clerk-hire allowance.

The original intent of the 1975 change was to give junior senators assistance in meeting their committee responsibilities. But because there no longer is any limit on the number of staff that can be employed, a senator can use his legislative aides for either committee or personal staff work.

NOTES

1. Paul S. Rundquist, "Congress and Parliaments," *CRS Review,* March 1989, 32.

2. William L. Morrow, *Congressional Committees,* (New York: Charles Scribner's Sons, 1969), 52.

3. Harrison W. Fox, Jr., and Susan Webb Hammond, *Congressional Staffs: The Invisible Force in American Lawmaking* (New York: The Free Press, 1977), 15.

4. Ibid.

5. Ibid., 20.

6. Richard A. Baker, *The Senate of the United States: A Bicentennial History* (Malabar, Fla.: Robert E. Krieger, 1988), 89-90.

7. Robert C. Byrd, *The Senate, 1789-1989: Addresses on the History of the United States Senate* (Washington, D.C.: Government Printing Office, 1988), 538.

8. Baker, *The Senate of the United States,* 89-90.

9. Michael J. Malbin, "Delegation, Deliberation, and the New Role of Congressional Staff," in *The New Congress,* ed. Thomas E. Mann and Norman J. Ornstein (Washington, D.C.: American Enterprise Institute for Public Policy Research, 1981), 138.

10. Byrd, *The Senate, 1789-1989,* 550.

11. Ibid., 549.

12. Fox and Hammond, *Congressional Staffs,* 22.

13. Norman J. Ornstein, Thomas E. Mann, and Michael J. Malbin, *Vital Statistics on Congress, 1991-1992* (Washington, D.C.: Congressional Quarterly, 1992), 120.

14. Hedrick Smith, *The Power Game: How Washington Works* (New York: Random House, 1988), 282.

15. Harold W. Stanley and Richard G. Niemi, *Vital Statistics on American Politics,* 3rd ed. (Washington, D.C.: CQ Press, 1992), 265-267.

16. Ornstein, Mann, and Malbin, *Vital Statistics on Congress, 1991-1992,* 120.

17. Paul Dwyer, "Legislative Branch Appropriations for Committee and Personal Staff and Agency Contributions: FY 1960-FY 1984," Congressional Research Service report, February 14, 1984.

18. Norman J. Ornstein, Thomas E. Mann, Michael J. Malbin, Allen Schick, and John F. Bibby, *Vital Statistics on Congress, 1984-1985* (Washington, D.C.:

American Enterprise Institute for Public Policy Research, 1984), 132; and Ornstein, Mann, and Malbin, *Vital Statistics on Congress, 1991-1992,* 140.

19. Ornstein, Mann, Malbin, Schick, and Bibby, *Vital Statistics on Congress, 1984-1985,* 135; and Ornstein, Mann, and Malbin, *Vital Statistics on Congress, 1991-1992,* 142.

20. Stephen Isaacs, "The Capitol Game," *Washington Post,* February 16, 17, 18, 19, 20, 22, 23, 24, 1975.

21. House Subcommittee on Legislative Branch Appropriations, *House Legislative Branch Appropriations Hearings for Fiscal 1991,* 101st Congress, 2nd sess., 1990, 90, 92.

22. Ornstein, Mann, and Malbin, *Vital Statistics on Congress, 1991-1992,* 128, 129.

23. Smith, *The Power Game,* 284, 289-290.

24. Ibid., 285.

25. Malbin, "Delegation, Deliberation, and the New Role of Congressional Staff," 170.

26. Fox and Hammond, *Congressional Staffs,* 43-46.

27. Richard E. Cohen, "The Hill People," *National Journal,* May 16, 1987, 1172.

28. Malbin, "Delegation, Deliberation, and the New Role of Congressional Staff," 151.

29. Kenneth Kofmehl, *Professional Staffs of Congress* (West Lafayette, Ind.: Purdue Research Foundation, 1962), 212.

30. Fox and Hammond, *Congressional Staffs,* 27.

31. Michael J. Malbin, *Unelected Representatives: Congressional Staff and the Future of Representative Government* (New York: Basic Books, 1980), 170-187.

32. Jeffrey H. Birnbaum and Alan S. Murray, *Showdown at Gucci Gulch: Lawmakers, Lobbyists, and the Unlikely Triumph of Tax Reform* (New York: Vintage Books, 1987), 217, 214.

33. Smith, *The Power Game,* 282.

34. Mark Bisnow, *In the Shadow of the Dome: Chronicles of a Capitol Hill Aide* (New York: William Morrow, 1990), 76.

35. Roger H. Davidson and Walter J. Oleszek, *Congress and Its Members,* 3rd ed. (Washington, D.C.: CQ Press, 1990), 138.

36. Fox and Hammond, *Congressional Staffs,* 49.

37. Richard F. Fenno, Jr., *The Emergence of a Senate Leader: Pete Domenici and the Reagan Budget* (Washington, D.C.: CQ Press, 1991), 4-5.

38. Bisnow, *In the Shadow of the Dome,* 131.

39. Ibid., 91.

SELECTED READINGS

Birnbaum, Jeffrey H., and Alan S. Murray. *Showdown at Gucci Gulch: Lawmakers, Lobbyists, and the Unlikely Triumph of Tax Reform.* New York: Vintage Books, 1987.

Bisnow, Mark. *In the Shadow of the Dome: Chronicles of a Capitol Hill Aide.* New York: William Morrow, 1990.

Byrd, Robert C. *The Senate, 1789-1989: Addresses on the History of the United States Senate.* Washington, D.C.: Government Printing Office, 1988.

Chaleff, Ira, Burdett A. Loomis, Gary D. Serota, and James A. Thurber. *Setting Course: A Congressional Management Guide.* 3rd ed. Washington, D.C.: American University, 1988.

Cooper, Joseph, and G. Calvin Mackenzie. *The House at Work.* Austin: University of Texas Press, 1981.

Cummings, Frank. *Capitol Hill Manual.* 2nd ed. Washington, D.C.: Bureau of National Affairs, 1984.

Davidson, Roger H., and Walter J. Oleszek. *Congress and Its Members.* 3rd ed. Washington, D.C.: CQ Press, 1990.

Dwyer, Paul E. "Salaries of Members of Congress: Congressional Votes, 1967-1989." Congressional Research Service, March 3, 1989.

Fenno, Richard F., Jr. *The Emergence of a Senate Leader: Pete Domenici and the Reagan Budget.* Washington, D.C.: CQ Press, 1991.

——. *Home Style: House Members in Their Districts.* Boston: Little, Brown, 1978.

——. *The Making of a Senator: Dan Quayle.* Washington, D.C.: CQ Press, 1989.

——. *The Presidential Odyssey of John Glenn.* Washington, D.C.: CQ Press, 1990.

Fiorina, Morris P. *Congress: Keystone of the Washington Establishment.* 2nd ed. New Haven, Conn.: Yale University Press, 1989.

Fox, Harrison W., Jr., and Susan Webb Hammond. *Congressional Staffs: The Invisible Force in American Lawmaking.* New York: The Free Press, 1977.

Francis, Charles C., and Jeffrey B. Trammell, eds. *The Almanac of the Unelected: Staff of the U.S. Congress.* 2nd ed. Washington, D.C.: The Almanac of the Unelected, 1989.

Jones, Charles O. *The United States Congress: People, Place, and Policy.* Chicago: Dorsey, 1982.

Jones, Rochelle, and Peter Woll. *The Private World of Congress.* New York: The Free Press, 1979.

Kofmehl, Kenneth. *Professional Staffs of Congress.* West Lafayette, Ind.: Purdue Research Foundation, 1962.

Malbin, Michael J. "Delegation, Deliberation, and the New Role of Congressional Staff." In *The New Congress,* edited by Thomas E. Mann and Norman J. Ornstein. Washington, D.C.: American Enterprise Institute for Public Policy Research, 1981.

——. *Unelected Representatives: Congressional Staff and the Future of Representative Government.* New York: Basic Books, 1980.

"Members' 1989 Honoraria Receipts," *Congressional Quarterly Weekly Report,* June 2, 1990.

"Members' 1990 Honoraria Receipts," *Congressional Quarterly Weekly Report,* June 22, 1991.

Miller, James A. *Running in Place: Inside the Senate.* New York: Simon and Schuster, 1986.

Morrow, William L. *Congressional Committees.* New York: Charles Scribner's Sons, 1969.

Parker, Glenn R. *Characteristics of Congress: Politics and Congressional Behavior.* Englewood Cliffs, N.J.: Prentice-Hall, 1989.

Redman, Eric. *The Dance of Legislation.* New York: Simon and Schuster, 1973.

Reid, T. R. *Congressional Odyssey: The Saga of a Senate Bill.* New York: W. H. Freeman, 1980.

Smith, Hedrick. *The Power Game: How Washington Works.* New York: Random House, 1988.

Smith, Steven S., and Christopher J. Deering. *Committees in Congress.* 2nd ed. Washington, D.C.: CQ Press, 1990.

Wolpe, Bruce C. *Lobbying Congress: How the System Works.* Washington, D.C.: Congressional Quarterly, 1990.

INDEX